WRITERS AND THEIR WORK

ISOBEL ARMSTRONG
General Editor

SHASHI DESHPANDE

T0338970

SHASHI DESHPANDE

Amrita Bhalla

NORTHCOTE

BRITISH
COUNCIL

First published in 2006 by Northcote House Publishers Ltd, Horndon, Tavistock, Devon, PL19 9NQ, United Kingdom.
Tel: +44 (01822) 810066. Fax: +44 (01822) 810034.

British Library Cataloguing-in-Publication Data
A catalogue record for this book is available from the British Library

ISBN 0-7463-1135-4 hardcover
ISBN 0-7463-0947-3 paperback

Typeset by TW Typesetting, Plymouth, Devon
Printed and bound in the United Kingdom by Athenaeum Press Ltd.

For my parents
Kiran and Sarwan Lamba

Contents

Acknowledgements

I am grateful for the help and encouragement of Gurmit and Kartar Bhalla, Gurmeet and Reecha Lamba, Vivek and Simrita Kamra, Naju Seth, Payal Gupta, Ritu Menon, Shernaz Cama and Makarand Paranjape. I would like to thank the British Council, especially Margaret Meyer for the assistance provided. Dr Deshpande and Shashi Deshpande's invaluable friendship gave me the confidence to carry on. Above all, my thanks to Jugnu, Saachi and Revant whose love, support, encouragement and patience made this book possible.

Biographical Outline

1938   Born 19 August in Dharwad, India, second daughter of Professor R. V. Jagirdar and Sharada Jagirdar.

1943–8   Schooling in St Joseph's School, Dharwad.

1948   Father resigns job in Karnatak College, Dharwad, and changes name to Adya Rangacharya.

1948–52   Schooling in Basel Mission Girls' High School, Dharwad.

1952   Joins Karnatak College, Dharwad.

1954   Father takes up job in Delhi. Joins Elphinstone College, Bombay.

1956   Graduates in Economics and Politics.

1956   Moves to Bangalore when father joins All India Radio, Bangalore.

1957   Joins Government Law College, Bangalore.

1959   Graduates in Law.

1959–60   Works with a criminal lawyer in the High Court, Bangalore.

1961–2   Works for a law reporter.

1962   In December marries Dr D. H. Deshpande, who works in G. S. Medical College, Bombay. Moves to Bombay.

1964   Birth of first son, Raghunandan, in January.

1966   Birth of second son, Vikram, in October.

1968   Husband awarded a Commonwealth Fellowship. Accompanies husband with children to stay in London for a year.

1969–70   Attends the Bharatiya Vidya Bhavan College of Journalism.

1970   Works briefly for magazine *Onlooker*. Writes first short story 'The Legacy' for the *Onlooker Annual*.

1970–75 A number of short stories published in various magazines.

1975   Husband resigns from job in Bombay and joins the National Institute of Mental Health and Neurosciences, (NIMHANS) Bangalore. Family moves to Bangalore.

1978   First short-story collection, *The Legacy and Other Stories*, published by Writers Workshop.

1980   *The Dark Holds No Terrors*, her first novel to be published.

1981   Husband gives up job in NIMHANS and starts his own consulting practice and pathological laboratory. She works for a year with husband.

1984   Wins an award for *Roots and Shadows*.

1984   Father's death.

1984–5 Works on completing untranslated chapters of father's translation of the Natyashastra into English.

1988   *That Long Silence* published by Virago Press, London.

1990   Receives the Sahitya Akademi award for *That Long Silence*.

1990   Writes script for film *Drishti* which wins a national award.

1991   Works on revising and editing father's work on the Bhagvad-Gita, later published as *The Quest for Wisdom*.

1991   Wins an award for *The Dark Holds No Terrors*.

1992   Marriages of both sons.

1993   *The Binding Vine* published.

1994   Birth of grandson Ajit.

1996   *A Matter of Time* published.

2000   Publication of *Small Remedies*.

2003   *Collected Stories*, vol. 1 published by Penguin India.

Abbreviations and References

BV   *The Binding Vine* (New Delhi: Penguin India, 1993)

DNT   *The Dark Holds No Terrors* (New Delhi: Penguin India, 1990)

LS   *That Long Silence* (New Delhi: Penguin India, 1989)

MT   *A Matter of Time* (New Delhi: Penguin India, 1996)

SR   *Small Remedies* (New Delhi: Penguin India, 2000)

1

Introduction

Yes, I did and I do write about women. Most of my writing comes out of my own intense and long suppressed feelings about what it is to be a woman in our society, it comes out of the experience of the difficulty of playing the different roles enjoined on me by society, it comes out of the knowledge that I am something more and something different from the sum total of these roles. My writing comes out of my consciousness of the conflict between my idea of myself as a human being and the idea that society has of me as a woman. All this makes my writing very clearly women's writing.

I have been put into the slot of woman writer, my writing has been categorized as 'writing about women' or feminist writing. In this process, much in it has been missed.

Now, after 26 years of writing I am able to define myself as a novelist and short story writer. I don't think any qualifying words are necessary – not Indian, not Indo-English, not woman, not feminist, not third world.[1]

The seemingly contradictory statements by Deshpande defining her position as a woman writer and then stating her dissatisfaction with the slot is a comment both on her works and on contemporary critical theory and literary criticism. Her statements defy the essentialist and reductive practices in current critical thought to label, structure, and direct to designated compartments the literature from decolonized nations. The eagerness to 'read' works by Indian writers as 'post-colonial' (in its many avatars) and Indian women writers as prescribing a homogenized 'feminism' is problematic; it demarcates analysis in ways that are limiting and stratified.

1

This totalizing tendency ignores and marginalizes contemporary indigenous culture even as strategically located theorists spin out definitions/preconceptions of 'Indian, Third World, (Indian) women'. The need to resist the hegemonizing and homogenizing claims of theory on the 'new literatures' of post-independence nations is increasingly felt. Theories that started out as well-intentioned, cultural tools historicizing the orientalist venture and analysing the construction of the binaries of 'centre' and 'margin' in an attempt to understand the marginalized, the 'other', the repressed and the silenced subaltern, acquired a Eurocentric, hegemonic status reinscribing the power of a 'voice' and 'knowledge'. Discourses studying the literary works in these overburdened, 'overworlded' sites need to be re-evaluated in the context of the contemporary dynamics of the location. The continual insistence on studying gender, too, in the context of colonialism is according an excessive import to a historical event. It is imperative to reassess and move away from the now anachronistic and facile nomenclature of post-colonialism.

Today, in the post-Rushdie era, even writers covered by the overarching rubric are probably wondering whether they are writing 'back', writing 'to', writing 'against' or within the parameters established by an overactive monolithic industry. Meenakshi Mukherjee's analysis of the literary and canonical failure of the early twentieth-century Indian novel in English in contrast to the international visibility and success of the novel in English in the last two decades may well be a statement on the novel today. Mukherjee suggests a self-consciousness of the novelist to 'explain' to a shadowy and indeterminate (international) reader the nuances of the 'civilizational essence of India': an 'assertion of a broadly *Indian* identity was undertaken generally to emphasize otherness and exoticity rather than to make a political statement'.[2] It seems as if theory and literature are equally implicated in creating a web in an international marketplace. Deshpande's statements, however, are the confident assertion of a writer who refuses to 'explain', 'exoticise' or defend her place as a woman writing in English in post-independence India, a multi-lingual, multi-religious, and multi-dimensional society of 360 languages and dialects. In literary studies today it would be a useful venture to make a paradigm shift from a study of a 'broadly Indian identity' constructed inevitably, or subtly suggested in theory as a binary, to a study of actual conditions in post-independence India. It is essential to locate and place Indian literary works in the context of the Indian 'society' that Deshpande speaks of, to deal with a specific location ever changing, vibrant, and mediated by its internal dynamics, the politics of its multi-polar binaries in terms of caste, class, gender, rural–urban divides and the myriad ways in which it functions. Aijaz Ahmad writes about the difficulties, or rather the impossibility or even the desirability, of explicating a cultural study of an evolving nation.[3] It would be useful to attend to the 'voice' of the Indian academic and writer whose analysis may contribute in manifold ways to our reading of literature but which may be at variance with canonized, formulaic, current methodologies. To this end, as an academic in India, I read the works of Deshpande in the context of (a) the women's movement in India, (b) a literary theory of Indian women writers, foregrounded against the western feminist literary theory with which Deshpande is familiar. I have suggested an approach that includes the perspective of the writer in the analysis of her work. Literatures in decolonized nations have been studied too exclusively in the light of the writings of Rushdie, Said, Bhabha and Spivak. Without discrediting their pioneering work in these fields the time has come to engage with the specific characteristics of the 'society' in which these works are written and studied before we enter the operational arena of drawing comparisons with or contentious issues against other societies.

GENDER AND PATRIARCHY

The central trope in Deshpande's novels, then, is the construction of Gender and Patriarchy in a society within which she places the conflict of her women protagonists. To suggest that there is a common definition of the way all societies are constructed in patriarchal terms that is valid for all times is simplifying, erasing difference and disregarding the particularities of individual nations as well as difference within national frameworks.

3

Feminists, particularly from the industrialized Western world, have been apt to make sweeping generalizations about commonalties among women across the globe. . . . Paradoxically, the very attempt to universalize feminism makes it more exclusionary.[4]

Women's identities have been shaped by varied factors specific to region, caste, class, and religion. Studies in India have reacted sharply to the presuppositions that claim that sisterhood is global and those that ignore women's issues in countries outside the US and western Europe. Amrita Basu states, in *The Challenge of Local Feminisms*, that it was the assumption of sameness which many assumed reflected an ethnocentric and middle-class bias that incurred the resentment of many 'Third World' women and generated deep divisions between women from the First and Third worlds at the UN conferences on women in Mexico City in 1975 and Copenhagen in 1980.[5] The divisions exist within a national framework and the societal, economic and cultural divide between, for example, an upper-caste Hindu woman and a tribal woman are legion. However, theoretical definitions are necessary, with qualification, for an understanding of the construct within which a system of male domination functions. Patriarchy would be defined as an organized system of control in which women are secondary, the 'other' in relation to the primary sex, subordinate to, suppressed, silenced and exploited by a society termed as 'patriarchal'. The word literally means the rule of the father and in most South Asian languages is termed accordingly: in Hindi, the language spoken by more than 600 million people, it is *pitrasatta*, in Urdu *pidarshahi*, *pitratontro* in Bengali and *pitruswamyam* in Telegu.

'Patriarchy has power from men's greater access to, and mediation of, the resources and rewards of authority structures inside and outside the home.'[6] The authority may be political, economic, cultural, religious, legal and manifest also in an institutionalized manner. In fact, in some Indian languages the term for husband suggests that he is 'lord and master': *swami*, *shauhar*, *pati*, *malik* would mean owner in all spheres. Kamla Bhasin identifies areas of subordination that include patriarchal control over (1) women's productive and labour power, (2) women's reproduction, (3) women's sexuality, (4) women's mobility, (5) property and economic resources. She states that the family teaches lessons in hierarchy and subordination. Motherhood is privileged as a role and the onus of parenting and nurturing is placed solely on the woman, creating stereotypes of male and female roles. The control over sexuality and mobility includes the imposition of 'purdah' and the restriction on leaving the domestic space is predicated on the myth of Sita crossing the threshold, falling prey to the lust of Ravana and thereby besmirching her character in the patriarchal state. The title of feminist studies like Malashri Lal's *The Law of the Threshold* (1995) and anthologies like *The Inner Courtyard* (1990) and Rabindranath Tagore's acclaimed novel *The Home and the World* (1919) suggest how deeply ingrained is the idea of inner and outer space, the sanctified private world and the dangerous world. Uma Chakravarti analyses the construction of a patriarchal Brahmanized society in terms of caste and gender hierarchies. The establishment of private property and the need for caste purity required strict control over a woman's mobility and sexuality. Patriarchy is successful when it is internalized as an ideology and observed by women as *pativrata* (wifely fidelity):

> whereby women accepted and even aspired to chastity and wifely fidelity as the highest expression of their self-hood. Because it was self-imposed, the hierarchical and inegalitarian social order was reproduced by the *complicity* of upper-caste women: their own subordinate status was successfully invisibilized and with it patriarchy was so firmly stablished as an ideology that it appeared to be natural.'[7]

In India, women were 'socialized into believing in their own *empowerment through chastity and fidelity;* through sacrifice they saw themselves as achieving both sublimation and strength. Thus they created a *strength out of their inferiority and weakness; through a rich and imaginative mythology women were narcoticized into accepting the ideology that genuine power lies in women's ability to sacrifice, in gaining spiritual strength by denying themselves access to power or the means to it.'[8]* The myths of Sita and Savitri provide a reference point for enforcing control. The norms of womanhood in specific terms have been fostered by recourse to religion, mythology, mass media, films and literature, oral and written texts. All major religions in India have been interpreted and controlled by upper-caste men who have also defined morality, social codes and ethics. A person's marriage, divorce and inheritance in India are determined by her religion. Religion codifies society in ways that privilege men.

A short historical survey of the construction and representation of Indian women from colonial times to the present may be useful in understanding the conflicting roles imposed on the contemporary Indian woman. Deshpande's work makes central the division between the stereotypifying and the reality of the urban middle-class, professional women in India today.

WOMEN IN NINETEENTH-CENTURY COLONIAL INDIA

The constitution of patriarchies in colonial India has been a subject of interdisciplinary work involving studies on the historical imperialist process that, in conjunction with or contradiction to traditional Indian society, governed the status of women. Understanding the reconstitution of patriarchies during colonialism and using gender as a mode of historical reconstruction impinges significantly upon the present. According to Sangari and Vaid, a feminist historiography of nineteenth-century colonized India is a significant tool in reconstructing the role of women freedom fighters: it discards the idea of women as something to be *'framed* by a context, in order to be able to think of gender difference as both structuring and structured by the wide set of social relations'.[9] Varied perspectives in art, literature and histories had shaped the image of Indian womanhood in the nineteenth century even as her avatar became a structured site for furthering vested interests. The orientalists privileged her as the repository of India's ancient glorious past, an amalgam of Brahmanical and Kshatriya values. The colonial administration and the Christian missionaries appropriated these studies and constructed a picture of the low status of Indian women to further their orientalist and political agenda of intervention into India's religious and indigenous laws. According to James Mill's *The History of British India*, Hindu women were in a state of dependence more strict and humiliating than that which is ordained for the weaker sex . . . Nothing can exceed the habitual contempt which Hindus entertain for their women . . . They are held in extreme degradation, excluded from the sacred books, deprived of education and (of a share) in the paternal property . . . That remarkable barbarity, the wife held unworthy to eat with her husband, is prevalent in Hindustan.[10]

With this indictment on the status of Indian women, the imperialists justified their colonial intervention into indigenous laws: Mrinalini Sinha discusses the axis of 'colonial masculinity' whereby the imperialists appeared as the protectors of Indian women, the Indian male was made effeminate and patriarchies were reconstituted.[11] The dynamics of gender relations were to be changed. In the colonialist venture, what was evoked again and again by the orientalists, Indologists and the Government was the notion of *pathivratha dharma* (worship of the husband). Lata Mani suggests that the legislation against Sati and Child Marriage, and the raising of the age of consent were part of the political agenda of the British, rather than a venture of reform for women.[12] The British imperialists, however, saw themselves as reformers whose purpose was to raise the status of Indian women. The position of the Indian women as perceived and projected by the Government and in colonial discourse served as a justification for legislation. The 'woman question' thus became a ground for political debate between the colonizers and the Indian male: certain patriarchal practices, however, were ratified and some disrupted. The treatment of women by Indian men was also used as a tool for dismantling political equality. The Ilbert Bill controversy brought to the forefront the fight between the Anglo-Indian 'memsahibs' and the Indian *bhadra mahila*. Sinha quotes a report of a British Deputy Commissioner: 'Is it seriously meant that natives who practice polygamy treat their wives as caged birds, kept in the dark chiefly for the creation of sons . . . who immolate infants of tender age to marriage, compel infant widows to remain widows till death – are as such competent to try European men and women?'[13] The Indian dissenters put forth their arguments about the achievements of the educated modern Indian woman, based on the fact that the University of Calcutta in 1878 admitted Indian women before any of the English universities.

In fact, the reconstruction and regeneration of the Indian woman became imperative in this debate. R. C. Dutt's *A History of Civilization in Ancient India* (1888) used the context of the Vedic woman for this purpose. Drawing his research from religious texts, he depicted her as 'the intellectual companion of her husband ... And as inseparable partners in their religious duties, Hindu wives receive the honour and respect due to their position'.[14] The Hindu woman also became the repository of an unsullied Indian purity in contrast to the Indian male who may have been educated in Western mores. The historical reconstruction of the Vedic woman and the ideal of Aryan womanhood were used as a norm also by women reformers, and organizations came to be known as Arya Mahila Samaj and Arya Nari Samaj. Thus, as Sinha says, 'the status of the Indian woman was made the site for competing political agendas, none of the opposing sides were interested in going beyond a narrow and self-serving model of female emancipation'.[15]

So what was the actual condition of women? How did they negotiate the binary between the traditional roles enforced on them by religious texts and social custom, and the demand made on them to participate in the freedom struggle? Emancipation was still required in areas of widow remarriage, child marriage, the age of consent, sati, polygamy, education and purdah.

Two first-person narratives – the autobiography of Rushsundari Debi, *Amar Jiban* (my life), 1868, and Pandita Ramabai's *The High Caste Hindu Woman* (1886) analyse the status of women in nineteenth-century India. Ramabai's account is devastating as it divides the life of a woman into three stages, childhood, married life and widowhood, each stage replete with sorrow and travails. In her analysis of the place of women in society, she states that women as mothers were honoured but as wives were classed with cows, female camels and slave girls. A wife mistreated by her husband had no rights outside her marital status. In fact women did not inherit their father's land and had no rights over the property of their husbands; they had no income of their own and even women of upper caste were economically dependent. Jotirao Phule, the nineteenth-century reformer of lower castes, bracketed the Brahmin woman with the *sudra* or lower castes as victims of patriarchal domination. As Tanika Sarkar points out, the standard domestic regulations included an early marriage before puberty so that the *garbhadhan* ceremony, or ritual cohabitation with the husband, would be performed as soon as the girl entered puberty. An indissoluble, non-consensual marriage with a man of any age, who could have more wives, meant a further oppressive set of rules and regulations.[16] A widow's lot was worse and her widowhood was considered a retribution for crimes committed in her previous life. Sati, in fact, was seen as a reprieve and release from a life of ignominy and harassment. Women were denied access to education and Rushsundari Debi's autobiography contains a moving account of her attempts to educate herself, defying social, religious and patriarchal strictures. William Adam's Second Report on the State of Education in Bengal, 1836, mentions the belief that a girl taught to read and write would soon become a widow and that education presupposed licentiousness.[17]

The situation needed reform, and the nineteenth century witnessed a major change in the status of women wrought not only by colonial legislation against sati (1829), child marriage, and age of consent, but also by movements by reformers and dissident religious sects like the Brahmo Samaj. These movements encouraged the woman's right to education, her right to divorce, and widow remarriage. This period saw major movements for *strishiksha*, women's education. Tanika Sarkar comments on the similarity between Raja Ramohun Roy and Mary Wollstonecraft, who felt that the difference in women's intellectual development was due to a difference in opportunity and not in innate nature. However, Sarkar reacts strongly to the suggestion of similarity between the education of Indian women and the Victorian women's emancipation.

The Victorian lady did not have to hide her literacy, she was not married off in her infancy, her husband could not be formally polygamous and the widow was not customarily barred from remarriage. Nor did she live in virtual seclusion. The reforms that Victorian feminists struggled for were not basic education, end to widow immolation, legalising widow remarriage, (widow-remarriage) de-legalising infant marriage.[18]

9

The first school for girls was started by British and American missionaries in the 1810s. The apprehension of the evangelical mission of these schools prompted the opening of Brahmo and Hindu schools for girls. The 'home' now represented the dead weight of tradition, and education went hand in hand with reform. The debate in this arena was whether education for women should be in English mores and customs or Indian traditions (Macaulay's intent was the propagation of the imperishable empire of arts, morals, literature and laws). On the other hand there was an outcry against anglicization. The women's issue, her emancipation and struggle, was contained within the polity of a colonized nation, now fraught with nationalist uprisings. Some schools stressed that education for women should be in the sphere of household accomplishments as the role of women as mothers was promoted by the Nationalists. Swami Vivekananda best expresses the role of the Indian woman and the crossroads she stood at by the end of the nineteenth century:

> There lie before her various strange luxuries . . . new manners, new fashions, dressed in which moves about the well educated girl in shameless freedom . . . Again the scene changes and in its place appear, with stern presence Sita, Savitri, austere religious vows, fastings . . . and the search for the self. On the one side is the independence of western society, on the other the extreme self-sacrifice of the Aryan society.[19]

The all encompassing roles that the Indian woman had to don included combining the mythic qualities of the suffering Sita, the faithful Savitri, the spiritual Maitreyi, the learned Gowri and the heroic Lakshmibai. She also had to participate in the nationalist struggle as a repository of traditional womanhood and indigenous nationhood.

On women, now, in the light of this historical background, rested the onus of the moral, spiritual upliftment of a nation governed by a foreign power and a reconstituted patriarchy, even as they were encouraged to participate in the political struggle for freedom. Undoubtedly there is a development in the status of women. The traditional role of a mother and a wife is now extended to a participation in a nationalist struggle.

WOMEN IN THE FREEDOM STRUGGLE

The success of the call given by Mahatma Gandhi to incorporate women in the freedom struggle rested on woman's avatar as a self-sacrificing, enduring, courageous being. 'If non-violence is the law of our being, the future is with women. Who can make a more effective appeal to the hearth than woman?' The role of women in the nationalist struggle towards the end of the nineteenth century was similarly problematized. Stereotypical feminine qualities were evoked as empowering: the licence to step out of the domestic sphere into the arena of nationalist politics in a codified society governed by strict religious texts and social pressures was daunting. Gandhi, called the parent of the Indian women's movement, achieved the impossible by again stressing the qualities of womanhood that were ratified by tradition and text. '*Ahimsa* means infinite love, which again means infinite capacity for suffering. Who but woman, the mother of man, shows this capacity in the largest measure? ... And she will occupy her proud position by the side of man as his mother, maker and silent leader.' Women had to participate and were required in the freedom struggle because they embodied the weapons of Gandhi – Ahimsa. Women were capable precisely because in moral power they were superior to men and by nature 'endowed with the quality of forgiveness', 'had hearts over-flowing with love', and 'were personification of the power of self suffering'. The point made by Gandhi was that representing purity, women would imbue the cause with glorification. 'No other proof of our struggle being one of self purification is needed than that lakhs of India's women are actively helping it.'[20] There seems to be a continuity of roles imposed on women to suit historical imperatives. It is interesting that the roles enjoined stressed the stereotypical female roles of homemaker, mother and wife: women were also enjoined never to lose sight of their traditional roles. They were empowered precisely because of their traditional roles.

Radha Kumar points out that the first half of the twentieth century saw the 'symbolic use of mother as a rallying device, from feminist assertions of women's power as mothers of the nation, to terrorist invocations of the protective and ravening mother goddess, to the Gandhian lauding of the spirit of endurance and suffering embodied in the mother'.[21] A connection was established between revolution, goddesses and Mother India. The goddesses Kali and Durga represented aspects of energy, nature and action – with both the protective and destructive aspects of *shakti*. The period saw a rise in Durga pujas and Kali, Durga and Chandi became the three eminent goddesses associated with nationalism. The participation of women in the freedom struggle and outside their homes was made easier with this association. Women represented unsullied purity, untainted by western mores and norms, and when educated, or through their association with these goddesses, became empowered to fight foreign powers. The nationalists extended the role of women as mothers and the definition of motherhood – women were mothers as homemakers, mothers of the nation, mothers of the future sons of the country. Sarojini Naidu in 1906 spoke assertively:

> I charge you restore to your women their ancient rights, for, as I have said, it is we, and not you, who are the real nation-builders . . . Educate your women and the nation will take care of itself, for it is as true today as it was yesterday and will be to the end of human life that the hand that rocks the cradle rules the world.

Motherhood was a major rallying point. Naidu said, 'It is suitable that I who represent the other sex, that is, the mothers of the men whom we wish to make men and not emasculated machines, should raise a voice on behalf of the future mothers of India'. In fact, 'women may form a sisterhood more easily because they are bound to every woman in the world by the common divine quality of motherhood'.[22] This semi-mystical vision of motherhood seems to be the defining picture of women in the early twentieth century. Norms were being established by men and women for this role. The emancipation of women was meant to be the emancipation of the nation, but other strategies of domination in a patriarchal society were contained. The attributes of womanhood were channelized to meet a cause that was invested with a higher ideology. All India women's organizations were established from around 1910 until the 1920s and served as forums for discussion and reform. The agenda of a meeting of the Bharat Mahila Parishad in 1905 ranged from 'The Hindu wife and what she should be', 'The place of women in modern India', 'The responsibilities of our sex', to 'Grahastha Dharma and Pativrata' (duties to home and worship of the husband). The inception of the women's movement can be traced not to a radical awakening but to a gradual enlightenment about the role to be played by women both in the home and in the nation. Their 'heroic role' was defined by reference to the past, mythic women and to contemporary freedom fighters Sarojini Naidu, Kamaladevi Chattopadhyaya, Aruna Asif Ali and Rajkumari Amrit Kaur. Each highlighted an aspect of the idealized Indian woman. Annie Besant glorified the self-sacrificing Hindu woman, Naidu the self-sacrificing Indian mother, and Kamaladevi the self-sacrificing peasant woman. However, contradictions abounded because the role of women activists was described and circumscribed. The dichotomy between the home and the outside world continued. Statements were made dissociating the women's movement from the western feminist movement, as the westernised woman became something to be shunned. The women's movement was subsumed in the movement for freedom, which would give women freedom and do away with all inequalities.

POST-INDEPENDENCE WOMEN

Just as the 'experience of colonial rule was one of the most important formative influences on the feminist movement of the twentieth century ... an equivalent influence on contemporary feminism has been the experiment of democracy in post-independence India'.[23] Gender was an important issue to a post-colonial nation and culture. The Constitution in independent India declared the equality of men and women and enjoined upon every citizen the duty to 'renounce any practice derogatory to women'. Proposals for radical changes in laws relating to marriage and succession culminated in the parliament passing four acts of the Hindu Code Bill – the Special Marriage Act, the Hindu Marriage Act, the Hindu Succession Act and the Adoption and Maintenance Act. The Bill raised the age of consent in marriage, gave women the rights to divorce, maintenance and inheritance, and treated dowry as *stridhan*. In the euphoria of freedom promises were made and administrative bodies established for improving the status of women. Women's issues in post-independence India were complex and made more complicated. Women's organizations during the colonial period had fought a common enemy without defining clear-cut gender issues. Freedom for the nation presupposed an equal status for women. The image of women changed – from the image of mother used as a rallying device in pre-independence India, to the symbol of woman as daughter and working woman in independent India. By focusing on woman as daughter the emphasis moved into a self-exploration of her role from girlhood to womanhood. A new subjectivity, according to Radha Kumar, was brought into Indian feminism, which expressed emotions that had not so far been stated. The focus also moved to women's productive rather than reproductive role. The emphasis on the economically independent working woman in free India has been seen as a demand not only for feminist assertiveness within the home, but also for a woman's right to control over her own body. As Kumar, in *The History of Doing*, says:

> So, from early nineteenth century definitions of the suffering of Indian women and the need for reform, by the early twentieth century the emphasis had shifted to stressing women's right to be treated as useful members of society, and by the late twentieth century to demanding that women should have the power to decide their own lives. Putting it another way, it can be argued that over the last one hundred and eighty years, the focus of campaigns for an improvement in women's lives has changed from needs to rights and within this from the restricted right to parity in selected areas to the larger right of self-determination'.[24]

The issues of self-definition and self-determination and the ensuing conflicts in a complex society have been depicted in the arts – cinema, print and electronic media, literature and painting. While the contemporary Indian women's movement is complex and encompasses a range of issues relating to work, wages, civil rights, sex, violence, representation, caste, class and health, the self-definition of the middle-class urban woman is further problematized. She lives in a society where tradition is an integral part of daily life and enjoins codes of cultural behaviour. The actualization of a self and identity is counterpointed against the established norms of a patriarchal society.

How does one assess the situation of middle-class urban women in contemporary India? Studies by Indian academics have sought to locate women's issues in their specific context and have marked departures from western feminism. Vrinda Nabar, in her *Caste as Woman*, discusses 'female awareness' in specific Indian situations, and titles her first chapter 'Our Women, Their Women'.[25] Malashri Lal in *The Law of the Threshold: Women Writers in Indian English* states that feminism with its Western connotations is a suspect term in India, seen as a disruptive force, and thought to be anti man and anti family. The problem, Lal feels, is with the nomenclature rather than belief, and that 'women's studies' is a more acceptable term for examining gender issues.[26]

In this context it would be useful to examine the role of theory in literary criticism and its validity as a tool of analysis for the works of Shashi Deshpande. Having studied the 'representation' of women in colonial and post-independence India and the 'role' enjoined on her by historical and traditional imperatives, I turn to literature and the question of an 'Indian feminist literary theory'. Before studying the terrain of Indian literary theory, I would like to examine the established theories relating to the arena of a post-colonial nation, women in post-colonial nations and the symbiotic link established between post-colonialism and feminism.

POST-COLONIALISM AND FEMINISM

The paradigm of Virginia Woolf's 'room of one's own' and economic independence as a necessary prerequisite for literary creativity has been disputed by black feminist writers. Alice Walker's *In Search of our Mothers' Gardens* (1984) has condemned the exclusive preserve of feminist critical theory as representing a white middle-class reality. The black feminist writers seek to address this lacuna which has 'disenfranchized', made deviant and excluded their literary works and experience from what they term mainstream, normative feminist, literary critical texts. These texts and theories have set up norms for an examination of only white, middle-class, female literature and experience/culture and do not provide a framework for black and Third World women writers. Deshpande in informal conversations has told me of the many times she would be writing her works on the dining table while supervising her children's meals. Vikram Chandra remembers his mother as 'she sat always at (her) dining table, writing in Hindi on long foolscap sheets of paper'.[27] The specificity of the local conditions of non-white women's writings has been ignored. Elaine Showalter in the path-breaking, *A Literature of Their Own* (1977), declared that 'we need to see the woman novelist against the backdrop of the women of her time, as well as in relation to other writers in history'.[28] The 'women novelists' examined by established canonical critical texts have been 'British women novelists from Brontë to Lessing' (the subtitle of Showalter's *A Literature of Their Own*). Ellen Moer's *Literary Women* (1976), Patricia Myer Spack's *The Female Imagination* (1975), and Sandra Gilbert and Susan Gubar's *The Mad Woman in the Attic* (1979) have been narratives of white female literary history.

Audre Lorde has written about the marginalization of black women and the 'minority discourse' that deals with the pejorative stereotyping of black women.[29] Barbara Smith's *Towards a Black Feminist Criticism* (1977) and Deborah E. McDowell's *New Directions for Black Feminist Criticism* (1980) address the issue and set about resurrecting forgotten Black women writers and correcting critical opinions of them since as Smith says 'without a Black feminist critical perspective not only are books by Black women misunderstood, they are destroyed in the process'. 'Until a Black feminist criticism exists we will not even know what these writers mean.'[30] Critics like Gloria Hull suggest the use of the term 'Black women's studies' as a political act, enabled by black feminist analysis. It is with the same intent that literary critics have addressed the issue of post-colonialism and feminism.

Recent post-colonial anthologies have included a section on post-colonialism and feminism, drawing attention to the similarities in discourses of domination/subordination, the gender/race divide, the politics of oppression/resistance and the concern for the marginalized. Introductions to these sections have also focused on the 'double colonization' of women in formerly colonized nations – both by imperialist and patriarchal societies. The strands of feminism and post-colonialism intersect in complex ways: 'Feminism has highlighted a number of the unexamined assumptions within post-colonial discourse, just as post-colonialism's interrogations of western feminist scholarship have provided timely warnings and led to new directions.'[31] However, literary critics like Ketu Katrak, Sara Suleri, Chandra Talpade Mohanty and Gayatri Spivak have criticized the levelling, and the homogenization of post-colonial theory and the attempt to elide post-colonialism and feminism and the feminism of Asian/black communities with western feminism. Their objections have stressed the limitations of Eurocentric models and theories generated for the examination of post-colonial texts even while excluding the interviews and essays of post-colonial writers. They have criticized the endless discussions of 'other' and 'difference' delineated in a complicated obscure language that ended up privileging the very scholar whose intention was to dismantle hegemonic structures. The objections have centred mainly on the production of monolithic, homogenized one-dimensional theories created without reference to actual conditions or subjects. Mohanty's 'Under Western Eyes: Feminist Scholarship and Colonial Discourses' (1984) is an excellent discussion on the many ways in which western feminist texts deal with Third World women. She writes that 'the assumptions of privilege and ethnocentric universality on the one hand, and inadequate self consciousness about the effect of western scholarship on the "third world" in the context of a world system dominated by the West, on the other, characterize a sizable extent of Western feminist work on women in the third world'. The construction of a monolithic, cross-culturally singular concept of patriarchy correspondingly leads to the creation of a reductive notion of a Third World woman. These assumptions and the uncritical use of methodologies also result in a singular notion of the oppression of women as a group. 'This average third world woman leads an essentially truncated life based on her feminine gender (read: sexually constrained) and her being "third world" (read: ignorant, poor, uneducated, tradition bound, domestic family oriented, victimized).' The binary delineated is with the self-representation of the western women not only as educated, liberated and free but also as the referent and norm. The representation of Third World women and the self-presentation of western women becomes the axis of analysis. Mohanty expresses the need to give voice to 'the overwhelming silence about the experiences of women in these countries'.[32]

WOMEN'S WRITING IN INDIA

The introduction to the ground-breaking two-volume anthology *Women Writing in India: 600 B.C. to the Present*, edited by Susie Tharu and K. Lalita, draws attention to these concerns and defines a methodology for an analysis of women's texts. The recovery of narratives by women from 600 BC to the present is a testimony to the rich literary heritage of India. In criticizing stereotypical depictions of women and in advocating the necessity to evolve analytical tools to address women's issues, Tharu and Lalita acknowledge the import of western feminist criticism in privileging women's writing; yet at the same time these authors warn against the trap that this framework for analysis invariably falls into:

> Tasks have been assigned, themes located, areas of debate defined, and women's writing authoritatively established as an object for disciplined investigation. The confidence of having drawn up no less than a world picture of the history of women's literature rings through the introduction of Elaine Showalter's 1985 collection of essays . . . the claims are awesome; the tone, one that colonized peoples have heard on many earlier occasions.[33]

The venture to mark out and stake women's writing as an area of study and to formulate analytical tools presupposes a common literary heritage. Showalter's statement that we now have 'a coherent, if still incomplete, narrative of female literary history, which describes the evolutionary stages of women's writing during the last 250 years' makes a claim that Tharu and Lalita cannot agree with.[34] They delineate four elements to bear in mind when studying women's literature in India. (1) The theme of loss and exclusion, of lost women writers and exclusion from the canon. (2) The notion of release or escape – they criticize the assumptions underlying Gilbert and Gubar's scheme whereby as the woman writer struggles for release she redefines her self and with it her social structure. Tharu and Lalita claim that what is defined by this paradigm is a Euro-American social history. (3) The concept of experience and the privileging of experience as the authentic source of truth and meaning – the critique of patriarchy, for example, only drew on the experience of middle-class feminism in the West. Patriarchy as historically constituted by class, colonialism and caste that would determine experience and selfhood in India was not addressed by western feminist literary theory and would be an important tool for analysis. (4) The hidden politics of what certain elements of western feminism have set out as women's real experience, or female nature. In the reconstitution of gender, western feminism assumed certain significations of their society as given, and did not critique notions of race and imperialism.

Tharu and Lalita say, 'we must also explore why it is that if we simply apply the theories of women's writing that have been developed over the last decade or so to women's writing in India, we will not merely reproduce its confusions but compound them'.[35] They are also aware of the dangers of homogenizing the experience of women in India – patriarchal practices and gender construction is created by specific region, class, caste and religion. 'Given the specific practices and discourses through which individualism took historical shape in India, the [non-white races, *dalits* (lower caste), underprivileged and minorities] had to be defined as Other in order that the self might gain identity.' The anthology then creates a context within which these works can be read, and sees them 'as documents that display what is at stake in the embattled practices of self and agency, and in the making of a habitable world, at the margins of patriarchies reconstituted by the emerging bourgeoisies of empire and nation'.[36]

Tharu and Lalita's introduction and biographical head notes to the women's texts may be regarded as a significant step in creating a literary feminist framework of analysis. They emphasize the reading of women's texts in the context of their

19

political and cultural background. For example, they place women's writing in the context of the restructuring of gender and patriarchy that was taking place in the nineteenth and early twentieth century (discussed at the beginning of this chapter). Twentieth-century women's writing is placed in the context of the 'major reorientation in the social Imaginary that took place as the Indian state set up its authorities in the forties and fifties, and as new movements of opposition emerged in the seventies'. Tharu and Lalita stress the history of 'contest and engagement' women's writing undertook. 'With what cunning did they press into service objects coded into cultural significations indifferent or hostile to them?' and 'how did they tread their oblique paths across competing ideological grids?' are the questions Tharu and Lalita would ask in reading women's texts.[37]

The counterpointing of tradition and modernity is one of the tools of analysis used by Lakshmi Holmström in her introduction to a collection of women's stories, *The Inner Courtyard*. She reads the stories as dealing with 'overlapping worlds of experience (for example, the world of myth and fantasy and the world of high technology; the world of traditional ritual and observance and a "modern" skeptical world; the world of collective responsibilities and obligations and the world of the individual)'. Holmström examines women's narratives in the context of the conflict between two worlds: 'what is of interest is the tension or negotiation between such worlds and the sudden sharp slippage from one into another'.[38] This binary between two worlds is one of the major conflicts portrayed in Deshpande's work. The concept of two diametrically opposed worlds is the subject of further studies.

A methodology for women's studies in India is defined in Malashri Lal's *The Law of the Threshold: Women Writers in Indian English*. She delineates the law of the threshold as a 'methodological resource for feminist literary criticism in India'. The threshold suggests the barrier between the inside – the arena of home and tradition – and the outside, associated with the world of men, business trade and politics. While men have passed over the threshold and can exist in both the worlds, the women are expected to inhabit only the space of home. 'For women, a step over the bar is an act of transgression. Having committed that act, they may never re-enter their designated first world and must live by their irretrievable choice of making the other world their permanent space.'[39] The woman conditioned by religion and social practice was designated the *Griha Lakshmi* (the prosperity of the household), 'a term that cunningly juxtaposes women's deification and her confinement in domestic space'.[40] The 'law of the threshold' then 'examines female destiny in India and its expressions in literature through *woman positioned in a real historical and social community context containing oppositional ideas of tradition for men and women*'.[41] While agreeing that Indian women cannot be homogenized (a point also made by Tharu and Lalita) and that it would therefore be 'erroneous to propose a uni-dimensional theory', Lal presents the law of the threshold as an Indocentric methodology that may be used as an analytical tool for women's writing in India.

Deshpande's essays, interviews and non-fictional writings provide an invaluable methodology for reading her works. Her statements have been interwoven in the chapters on her books.

ON WOMEN

Deshpande looks at constructions of womanhood specifically in the context of the social and cultural conditions that exist in India – the oral tradition of telling stories based on our epics and puranas, plays, dances, songs, poems, jokes, movies and tele-serials. She sees myths as a referral point in our lives, internalized and part of our psyche, 'part of our personal, religious and Indian identity':

> How we see ourselves collectively or individually, depends greatly on myths. They are part of the human psyche, part of our cultural histories. The myths present role models and images that women are expected to adhere to: 'to be as pure as Sita, as loyal as Draupadi, as beautiful as Laxmi, as bountiful a provider as Annapoorna, as dogged in devotion as Savitri, as strong as Durga' – these are all the ultimate role models we cannot entirely dismiss ... the examples are it seems held out only to women. It seems odd that it took us women so long to realize this truth, to understand why this is so.[42]

21

It is this realization of a concept of womanhood specific to religious, cultural and social practices in India that Deshpande explores in her work. She gives voice to women who in their explorations step out of the stereotypical roles formulated within patriarchal practices. Her novels are imbued with references to myths; however, now it is the women's perspective of them. The privileging of what women are rather than what they ought to be, a fancy constructed by men, is Deshpande's point of view. 'We will not bear any guilt that we cannot [approximate to the pictures of ideal womanhood]. More important than knowing what we are not is to know what we are, what is possible for us.' As a writer Deshpande claims that she is seeking knowledge, retelling the old stories: 'yes, women writers are now exploring the myths and stereotypes . . . what women writers are doing today is not rejection of the myths but a meaningful and creative reinterpretation of them'. Deshpande gives voice to the 'stone women', archetypal of the flattening, one-dimensional depiction of women by men: she makes gender central, the organizing principle of the lives of women. Her protagonists are middle-class professional urban women walking the tightrope of tradition and modernity, negotiating the balance between the spaces within and outside the threshold.

Deshpande locates the notion of feminism in her specific context: 'feminism, I read somewhere, is a movement that has grown out of and built upon prevailing social needs. I can see how true this is in India, where it has grown out of our own society, out of local specific issues and has addressed them directly.'[43]

It is appropriate to start an analysis of Deshpande's work by relating her sentiments on the way writers have been analysed.

What we need at present are critics who can put our writing in the right context – which is here. It is certainly not wrong for a critic to use literature written and published outside the country as a reference point, but to make it the only reference point is ridiculous . . . our writing comes out of this society, the emotional bonds are here . . . it is critics who need to widen their understanding to learn to contextualise correctly, to shake off the vestiges of colonialism that makes them ignore the distinctiveness of our writing. In other words, we need to see ourselves with our own eyes.[44]

Deshpande's work may then be situated in the context of the complexities in the construction of Indian womanhood as reflected in (a) the specific historical conditions of the women's struggle in India and the way women were represented, (b) a literary theory based on specific cultural/social/religious contexts, the significance of the threshold for example, (c) Deshpande's interviews and essays discussing the conflict of the urban woman structured by tradition and modernity.

2

The Dark Holds No Terrors

> The fact is that we do not start with a picture of ourselves
> on a clean slate. There are things told to us by others,
> things we have read, imagined and dreamt.[1]

The Dark Holds No Terrors, first published in 1980 by Vikas
Publishers and then by Penguin India, 1990, tells the story of
Sarita (Saru) – the movement backwards and inwards is
towards her engagement with her self, an attempt to clear the
'picture', to erase the conception of a self image as well as to
re-examine an image constructed by 'others'. The self is central
to the venture; the purpose is to know her self not in isolation
but in relation to her family and society.

Deshpande says that it was only when she wrote *The Dark
Holds No Terrors*, after contributing short stories to women's
magazines, that she felt a sense of satisfaction. 'The theme of
the liberated woman had been a germ inside me for a long
time. I had started with the short story "A Liberated Woman".
It seems to me when I finished this novel that I had come close
to what I had wanted to write.'[2] She says that it was 'a serious
novel about a serious human predicament',[3] and she never
thought of it as only a woman's novel: 'It was difficult to write,
it was different from the other novels I had read written by
Indian writers ... but all the reviews that came spoke of it as
a novel about a woman, a middle class woman, a professional
woman etc. In effect, a novel about a woman'.[4] Deshpande
identifies *The Dark Holds No Terrors* as the novel that gave her
a voice and her subject: 'my kind of writing came to me
through this novel ... I found my voice in this novel and
moved away from short stories'.[5] Though it was a difficult
novel for her to write, it 'flowed out of her' because she

understood the problem faced by the woman protagonist, Saru.

The epigraph is taken from the *Dhammapada*, one of the fifteen important treatises of the Basket of Discourses, the teachings of the Buddha. Consisting of 423 Pali verses uttered by the Buddha, the *Dhammapada* may be termed 'The Way of Truth' and expounds the philosophical and moral teachings of Buddhism.[6] The epigraph places the onus of self-discovery and salvation on Saru.

Sarita, a professionally successful doctor, married to Manohar and the mother of two children, returns alone to her family home after her mother's death, for no apparent reason and for an unspecified period of time. Having stepped across the threshold as a young woman to marry the dashing poet Manohar, against the wishes of her mother, Saru re-enters the home and re-crosses the threshold. The return, a central trope in Deshpande's novels, facilitates a re-examination of past relationships, of all that has been told to her, dreamt or imagined by her and, more significantly, a review of her present circumstances – her identity as a working wife and mother and the immediate crisis that motivates this return, marital rape. The reader is hurled headlong into a scene of rape, the last line of the first chapter revealing the identity of the rapist – the victim's husband.

The reader is introduced to a supposedly happy family – two children, the ideal number in India (*Hum Do, Hamare Do*, the two of us and two of ours, is a slogan propagated by an aggressive family-planning campaign in a country of more than one billion people), an elegant, sophisticated, professionally successful wife of a supportive husband living in 'a paradise of matching curtains and handloom bedspreads'.[7] Saru's unannounced and sudden appearance at her father's doorstep recalls to her mind the Krishna–Sudama story, a parable from Indian mythology: childhood friends, Krishna and Sudama go their separate ways, Krishna to become the king of Dwarka and Sudama to a life of penury. Sudama appears at Krishna's gate with a small gift of puffed rice and finds on his return home, after a restful holiday and *without speaking* about his poverty, a palatial mansion. The parallels go beyond the similarity of Saru/Sudama knocking at the door –

Saru hopes, by some miracle and without saying anything, to find a changed situation when she returns to her marital home. Deshpande's novels are deeply rooted in Indian myth and legend: 'myths condition our ideas so powerfully that often it is difficult to disentangle the reality of what we perceive from what we learn of our selves through them. In India, myths are perhaps even more powerful, for they have been with us in a long and unbroken tradition. The myths continue to be a reference point for people in their daily lives and we have so internalized them that they are part of our psyche, part of our personal, religious and Indian identity.'[8] The Krisha Sudama myth would be widely known.

The family home as a space to revisit, to cross into after crossing out – even though 'the die was cast, the decision taken, my boats burned. There could be no turning back (*DNT* 37) – becomes a recurring symbol in Deshpande's novels, as Jaya in *That Long Silence* and Sumi in *A Matter of Time* also return to their natal homes. The movement back facilitates the counterpointing of past and present, another device of Deshpande, as her women protagonists contend with the examination of their identity, then and now. The house however is never depicted as a cocoon, a nurturing haven or a peaceful retreat. It is not a 'room of one's own' for creativity or mental space. The epigraph, 'you are your own refuge/ there is no other refuge', sets the tone for Saru's journey. The house, like the house in *A Matter of Time*, is like a character, with its internal dynamics specific to itself, subject to changes and fraught with memories of unresolved crises. It absorbs the tensions and the characters of its inmates: the binary of inner space/outer space, home/world, familiar/unfamiliar, refuge/ strange world is however not reflected in this house. There are no easy solutions in stepping back into the house. The rooms are replete with childhood memories and associated with gender consciousness and difference. The conditioning to subservience and inadequacy starts early in childhood when Saru is debarred from the *puja* room and kitchen for the three days of menstruation. The *puja* room is associated with a sense of shame with Saru, 'feeling a pariah with my special cup and my plate by my side in which I served from a distance, for my touch was, it seemed, a pollution. A kind of shame ...

26

engulfed me ... if you are woman, I don't want to be one' (*DNT* 62). (Mira, in *The Binding Vine* writes a poem on this sense of shame; both women, Saru and Mira, are also linked by the theme of marital rape.) The sacred space within the house – the puja room and kitchen – instil a religious and cultural code by which the woman is both pure and impure, mistress and pariah, care-taker and outsider. It is significant that with her mother's death Saru is given the puja room as just a room to sleep in. Her mother was a repository of religious and cultural codes, but Saru, having crossed the threshold, exists outside those codes now. Her parents' room similarly defines the 'space' given to women. 'It had been "their" room, but it had always seemed only his, so success-fully had she managed to efface her personality from the room' (*DNT* 19). Now when Saru re-enters the room it is to confront again the feeling of deprivation and inferiority she had experienced as a girl child, the mirror on the *almirah* reminding her of the time she thought she was ugly, the smell of mothballs, *attar* and rose-water reminding her of the puja she was allowed to perform on that rare occasion when she was more important than her brother. Past and present are compac-ted when even with the locking of the *almirah*, the closing of the room, and the new cooking implements in the kitchen, the changed dynamics of the house do not erase the past.

There are three houses in the novel – her father's house, the one-room *chawl* and the elegant home Saru now inhabits – each house underlining the way she is conditioned. Though the one-room *chawl* 'was heaven, inspite of the corridors smelling of urine' (*DNT* 40), it is here that Saru is made conscious of being a 'lady doctor'. The difference is made obvious here, as the door is open to a line of patients, the corridors filled with smiles, murmured greetings and *Namastes*, all for her, not for Manohar. The room is blamed for highlighting a situation whereby that which made her taller made him shorter, for privileging her as a professional over him when society expected her to follow him seven steps behind.

The return to her ancestral home gives Saru a sense of perspective, allowing her to see the constitution of a self conditioned by the voices of the other – mother and father verbalizing the weight of centuries of tradition. She discards every identity that defined her – now she is no longer wife, mother or professional woman. 'She was the wronged child again, the unloved daughter, the scapegoat' (*DNT* 182). But before becoming the child again, Saru contends with the counterpointing of the complete professional woman, the doctor ('no, not I, really, but the dummy in the white coat', *DNT* 23), with the notion of wifehood and motherhood transcribed through the ages, percolated through generations by myths, legends and social expectations. From the time of her definition as lady doctor, Saru sees a redefinition of her gender relationship with her husband. 'Now I was the lady doctor and he was my husband' (*DNT* 42). She had grown up with the concept of femaleness in relation to the superior conquering male, a notion informed through the ages of the man–woman relationship. 'I was all female and dreamt of being the adored and chosen of a superior, superhuman male . . . I saw myself humbly adoring, worshipping and being given the father–lover kind of love that was protective, condescending . . . there was no "I" then' (*DNT* 53). The success of the professional woman, working outside the house, recognized as an identity, distinct from, and more successful than the male, is underscored by feelings of guilt if the 'I' dared to overreach the male. The consciousness of the 'I', the construction of an identity, is always seen in the social context. Saru's identity as a doctor is never seen in isolation but always in relation to what Manohar is: she was the lady doctor and he was her husband, she was earning not only the butter, but most of the bread as well, more than him. 'Things told to us by others', 'things we have read', have informed us of the subservience–dominance binary built into the man–woman relationship. 'A wife must always be a few feet behind her husband. If he's an MA, you should be a BA. If he's 5' 4" tall, you shouldn't be more than 5' 3" tall. If he is earning five hundred rupees, you should never earn more than four hundred and ninety-nine rupees . . . Don't ever try to reverse the doctor–nurse, executive–secretary, principal–teacher role' (*DNT* 137). Deshpande places Saru's thoughts in the context of easily recognizable women in Indian myth – Draupadi and Sita and Kalidas's Shakuntala.[9] Overturning again the paradigm of economic independence and a room of one's own as necessary prerequisites for a woman's identity, Saru avers that even if Draupadi and Sita had been economically independent, their stories would not have been different. A lesson learnt by Sita and Draupadi was to surrender and consciously abandon independence. Women in myth were to be emulated for their acceptance and subservience, Saru feels. She sees herself as a victim of economic independence and tries to instil strategies of repression and subservience by pretending to be not as smart, competent, rational and strong as she really is. The modern Indian woman in post-independence India walks a tightrope between the traditional concepts of wifehood enfor-ced by myth and social codes and modern concepts of the professional women working outside the home. She attempts to cope with the guilt she feels because the fact that she has an identity of her own effectively whittles down that of Manohar, and she tries to deal with the pretence of being less than him. She is depicted as a woman experimenting with various strategies of survival in a social structure where the reversal of roles threatens traditional notions of manhood. She tries to abandon that role to become purely a wife and mother – an easily recognizable and acceptable role: 'live like the others do . . . stay at home and look after the children. Cook and clean . . . a mother in an ad, in a movie, dressed in a crisply starched, ironed sari. Wife and mother, loving and beloved. A picture of grace, harmony and happiness' (DNT 80).[10]

Deshpande introduces in the novel women constructed in stereotypical roles: Saru meets women from the neighbour-hood suffering from myriad complaints but silent about their maladies, kept secret, borne stoically, and a matter of shame to them – 'their unconsciousness, unmeaning heroism, born out of the myth of the self-sacrificing martyred woman' (DNT 107); (Mohan's mother and sister in That Long Silence similarly remain silent about their illness), she has women friends who to suit their roles as wives had schooled themselves to subservience, regression and silence; she hears about women who, ill-treated by in-laws had ended their silence by jumping into a well. The silences of women and their repression is a major theme that Deshpande examines in her portrayal of Jaya in That Long Silence, Mira in The Binding Vine and Kalyani in A Matter of Time. The notion of pativratha, chastity, fidelity and glorified motherhood, is disseminated and imbibed through recognizable myths and social structures.

Saru returns alone, not as wife or mother, to her father's house. The first step, it seems, in her journey of self-discovery is the discarding of the outer signs that made her an elegant, professional, successful woman. She reverts to a life of austerity, comforting in its parameters, living the way women she knew in her childhood lived – with two saris for 'home wear', hair tied practically in a knot, hands rough with housework. She also enters a world simpler in its definitions – the men went to work, crossing and re-crossing the threshold, the children to school, the women stayed at home, within the threshold, and cooked and cleaned, scrubbed and swept. The movement takes her away from a world made complex by the blurring of boundaries in gender relations. So Saru comes back and thus starts her journey to understand the darkness within and outside.

Meenakshi Mukherjee views Saru as a professional doctor who is able to 'analyze her physical and psychological trauma with the detachment of an analyst'.[11] Deshpande's novel is the first of her works that make central the reflections of a woman who distances herself from a stereotypical world to re-examine issues and to find a release. The writer examines, probably for the first time in the literary history of Indian women's writing in English, the issue of marital rape, a theme she had dealt with in her short story 'The Liberated Woman', and was to examine again in *The Binding Vine*.[12] The prelude to the first chapter describes in detail a scene of rape, with the last line revealing the identity of the rapist – the victim's husband.

Manohar, Saru's husband, was the man who was to take the literary world by storm, a poet, confident and self-assured, attractive and romantic. He provides her with the escape she needs from a restrictive home, and the darkness of her brother's death – the freedom and space that she needs. The man we see now is 'just another man, clinging to a job', a college lecturer, a husband for whom Saru loses respect as he quietly accepts her success and the assistance she takes from Boozie in achieving it. Significantly, the reader never hears Manu's voice, but sees him through Saru's perspective. The male characters in Deshpande's scheme (except for Gopal in *A Matter of Time*), from Mohan in *That Long Silence* to Kishore in

The Binding Vine to Som in *Small Remedies*, exist, as she says, 'in the wings'. Saru links Manu's emasculation to her own success: 'it is because I am something more than his wife that he has become what he is'. The symbiotic relation of man–woman is cast in strict stereotypical boundaries of dominance and subservience. Any change in the dynamics of the power balance, a change both encouraged by the evolving economic, social framework of modern India and discouraged by tradition, myth and legend informing that framework, destroys the relationship. Saru's success as a doctor makes her more than a wife, Manohar's relatively lower status, economic and social, makes him less than a husband: these distinctions, commented on by 'others', hold up a mirror to Manohar, who then enforces his superior 'rights' as a man.

Each incident of marital rape follows a predictable pattern – stemming from a comment or a conversation – ' "if you had married a doctor", the wife said tartly, "you'd have gone to Ooty too . . . London, Paris, Rome, Geneva' '' (*DNT* 111), by the 'other' highlighting the changed power dynamics of the husband–wife relationship. The façade of normality, cheerfulness and breakfast banter unerringly assumed by Manohar the morning after his terrifying savagery bewilder Saru. She notices a divided self, a fractured male identity. Is there an understanding of Manohar's actions, pre-empted as they are by damaging comments? Deshpande, however, makes a very definitive point by making the woman central to this examination. True, this is a human predicament, but now seen from the point of view of the woman. She gives a voice to the mythic 'stone women', and the many voiceless women who bear their darkness stoically. There have been too many instances she feels when 'a man must have written this story' and now women are 'telling their tales'. 'Writers in India in search of some truths about themselves and their condition invariably go to the epics and the Puranas. So do women. And when they began, they were in effect rediscovering themselves, finding things relevant to their lives today.'[13] Deshpande is a woman writing a story, Saru is a woman who does not write or speak, but needs to. Later – in *That Long Silence*, in *The Binding Vine* and in *Small Remedies* – Deshpande was to write about the import of ending a long silence and verbalizing or writing.

Saru's response to this ordeal is to go deeper into the darkness within, silenced and repressed. In a similar situation, Mira in *The Binding Vine* had expressed her self in writing both poems and a diary. Saru lacks both voice and a forum for self-expression. She quotes Betty Friedan saying that it was easier for her to start the women's movement than to change her personal life. But Saru stands in a line of Indian literary and mythic women before her who had schooled themselves to silence (see note 9 and the Sanskrit story, *DNT* 207). Though Saru decries her women patients for their silence, she herself exists in the darkness of the past while silent about the darkness of being an abused wife.

The past is encountered in its full force when Saru cannot escape the memories of her mother. The impacting of the past and the present is most evident when Saru unconsciously reflects her mother's gestures, expressions and words, and occupies her 'space': 'and she went on jumbling her self with the dead woman sometimes feeling she was acting out a role, sometimes feeling she was her mother her self'. Deshpande's heroines share a distant or troubled relationship with their mothers – Jaya in *That Long Silence* and Urmi in *The Binding Vine*; Sumi in *A Matter of Time* fears that her life should not reflect her mother's, while Munni in *Small Remedies* consciously rejects her mother. Deshpande, when asked in an interview about autobiography, acknowledges that 'certain things are autobiographical – a character, an idea. There's a certain intensity about them. Take, for example, Saru's feeling of not being a wanted daughter in *The Dark Holds No Terrors*. Some of that has come from my own life'.[14] Saru's mother had assumed the voice of patriarchy and enforced traditional gender biases in her house. Dhruva her son had been the centre of their world and Saru the unloved, unwanted daughter. The novel gives expression to the myriad ways the son is privileged over the daughter in Indian households. The bitterness of this gender consciousness is heightened in Saru's mind when Dhruva at age 7 drowns. Her mother's tirade against the girl unable to save her brother from death crystallizes in Saru's mind. 'Why didn't you die? Why are you alive and he dead . . . [you] killed him' (*DNT* 191). 'Things told to' Saru about her mother's bitterness towards her after she crosses the threshold to marry Manohar mark the final break. Dhruva's death is explained by Deshpande as inevitable. 'Dhruva's death was a vital part of Saru's experience. When he came to me, he came dead. At no point in my mind was he living. In fact, I had a lot of difficulty writing the scene of his drowning. I was drained by the time I finished'.[15]

The darkness within is compounded by a self-generated guilt about Dhruva's death, her mother's curses and the belief that the present crisis is a punishment she deserves. The release, almost at the end of the novel, occurs when Saru is able to speak, to voice the darkness within to her father. She speaks and relates to others, emerging from months and years of silence. Her father confides that silence had become a habit between him and his wife. 'Now . . . go on, tell me. Tell me everything' (DNT 199).

The trope of writing as an outlet, a major thread in Deshpande's later novels (Jaya writes in That Long Silence, Mira writes poems and Urmi transcribes them in The Binding Vine, Sumi writes a play in A Matter of Time, and Madhu in Small Remedies a biography), first finds expressions in The Dark Holds No Terrors as Saru speaks to her father about her guilt and terror. Her silence for so long, her inability to talk to anybody about her fears, shocks her father. Now, past and present coalesce as the darkness of the present is seen as an expiation for past sins: 'maybe I deserve it after all. Look what I've done to him. Look what I did to Dhruva. And to my mother. Perhaps if I go on suffering', (DNT 204). The breaking of the silence of the past and the present marks a release for Saru.

Deshpande says, 'I think a woman's story is about much more than victimisation'. Saru's strength lies in her decision to come out of her silence and speak. She is in charge of her life and consciously acts on her decision. She chooses to keep quiet and later chooses to speak. Deshpande says about Saru's voicelessness, 'one answer is Saru her self. She has learned to gag her self. Silence has been both the oppressor's infliction and women's strategies. What we want to reach at finally is the telling'. Saru is central to her world and takes the step to analyse and speak. Deshpande says about her women's characters who move away from their families to reflect and speak, 'it's not an end. It's a beginning. They've stripped themselves. Seen themselves. Bare. One starts from there. It's like rebirth to me'.[16] The process of confronting oneself and then 'telling' or writing is seen by Deshpande as a catharsis and a release.

Saru sees the truth about her mother and her husband after voicing her inner traumas. Deshpande acknowledges that her women stand alone at their moment of realization, but stand fulfilled: 'this aloneness is the only link between mother and daughter. There is no feeling, no communication between the two. At no point is there any sympathy ... there is no reconciliation. But there is this. This commonness. It's so important. So, such a beginning of life is not at all a vacuum. It's full and rich.'[17] The end of the novel is a new beginning for Saru. The title of the novel, which highlighted the 'terrors inside us all the time' and enforced the belief that 'the dark holds no terror' (*DNT* 85), is justified by the conclusion after Saru sees her self as she is, and begins with a 'clean slate'.

The Dark Holds No Terrors inaugurated Deshpande's consciousness as a serious writer, and the kind of novel she was to write later. The theme of this book was to be elaborated in *That Long Silence* and *The Binding Vine*, before Deshpande moved from the interiority and anger of these works to the 'outwardness' of *A Matter of time* and *Small Remedies*.

3

That Long Silence

> I see writing ... as a struggle. Like childbirth. You have to force it out of you. At the same time, you are ashamed of your body taking control over you. So you want to hold on as well. Writing is a kind of self-revelation.[1]

> What we are now doing is retelling our own tales.[2]

That Long Silence, first published by Virago Press, London, 1988, and then by Penguin India in 1989, deals with Jaya's self-realization; stripped bare of the construct of wifehood and motherhood, starting on a 'clean slate' she reflects on her identity of being a woman and of ending a long silence of repression in a traditional family through the process of writing.

A lifetime of introspection went into this novel and as with *The Dark Holds No Terrors* this marked a personal and literary watershed.

> With the writing of this novel I crossed another barrier. It was with this novel that I, as Naipaul says, 'defined myself through my work'. It was with the articulation of all that had been in me through the years that I came to feminism, to a consciousness of myself as a feminist. I read a great deal after this – Simone de Beauvoir, Germaine Greer, Betty Friedan, Kate Millet, Virginia Woolf ... But it was not these books that made me a feminist; they were only confirmatory. My idea of feminism came to me out of my own life, my own experiences and thinking.[3]

Deshpande identifies *That Long Silence*, as the most autobiographical of all her writings, 'not in the personal details but in the thinking and ideas'. She pinpoints specifically the autobiographical element:

There's Jaya's feeling that she has had to suppress the intellectual part of herself. She knows that she is a very intelligent young woman in a very conventional marriage; she wants to make that marriage a success, fit into the role of wife, so she cuts out those parts that do not fit. All that to some extent is autobiographical. The struggle not to reveal oneself in one's writing as in *That Long Silence* is partly autobiographical as well.[4]

Deshpande's statements express the significance of writing, specifically *That Long Silence*, as a means of self-realization and creativity for a woman writer. She locates the defining moment in her consciousness of her self as a feminist in her own experiences and thinking and in her specific world. Her woman protagonists also come to this knowledge, which to her 'is a great feeling . . . like drinking Asterix's magic potion. You feel full of power'.[5] Saru, in *The Dark Holds No Terrors*, reaches her nemesis through telling and verbalizing her anxieties; Jaya, in *That Long Silence*, in writing. The central concern then in *That Long Silence* is the paradox experienced by Deshpande: writing as self-discovery and knowledge in conflict with the attempt of the woman writer not to reveal herself, to practise restraint and control; writing as self-expression in conflict with the self-generated suppression of a woman who has to 'fit' her self to a preconceived image, 'cut' and repress her intellect to conform.[6]

The process of self-realization is located within the home itself, a point Deshpande repeats in her later novels. The trope of crossing the threshold or recrossing/revisiting acquires another dimension in this novel. Jaya, at a point of crisis in Mohan's life and by association hers – 'a pair of bullocks yoked together'[7] – relocates for an unspecified period, from an elegantly furnished home in a prosperous locality to the Dadar flat. She enters, 'stripped bare', as Deshpande describes her women protagonists, of all the paraphernalia of middle-class existence. Jaya had kept for her family – her husband, herself and two children – 'a carefully furnished home yoked to all the monsters that had ruled [her] life, gadgets that had to be kept in order, the glassware that had to sparkle, the furniture and curios that had to be kept spotless and dust-free' (*LS* 25). This home, a carefully constructed unit, like Saru's, is a validation of the dreams of success of a couple aspiring to acquire both

the gloss and the chimera of happiness portrayed in advertise-
ments – 'cosy, smiling, happy families in their gleaming homes
spelt sheer poetry . . . they were the fairy tales in which people
live happily ever after' (*LS* 3). The home is also carefully
constructed to contrast with the provincial childhood homes
both Mohan and Jaya had inhabited surrounded by grandmothers, aunts, uncles and cousins. Those homes were austere,
bare and hard, their rooms lifeless, with fading paper flowers,
stiff chairs and dead grandfather clocks. Or they were a chaotic
mess, with clothes piled high or flung on a string tied from
wall to wall, piled mattresses and unmade beds. But Jaya and
Mohan move to metropolitan Bombay to define their own lives
themselves, to create a home with all the trappings and
trimmings of upper-class existence, which would erase the
memories of a spartan childhood. This motivation of Mohan to
acquire a lifestyle – 'a well-educated, cultured wife' (*LS* 92)
with her hair cut short in a modern style, in a carefully
furnished home – brings trouble on his career, as he cannot live
on just his salary. The novel starts at this point of crisis when
the two move to the Dadar flat. Deshpande had wanted to
write about the change in people and their moral values from
the pre-independence Gandhian era to the post-1970s. Against
this backdrop, however, is Jaya – central to the novel and the
focus of the novel is Jaya.

Deshpande admits that, from the beginning, the novel is a
monologue by Jaya sitting within the four walls of her house.
There is no other voice, no other perspective, she says.
Deshpande admits to years of turmoil in her personal life after
The Dark Holds No Terrors when, in a different set of circumstances, she found herself sitting at home, as confined as Jaya is. She
realized that this novel was about silences, the huge silences
which surround women's lives and which they surround
themselves with. This lay like a huge weight on her heart. The
epigraph 'If I were a man and cared to know the world I lived
in, I almost think it would make me a shade uneasy – the
weight of that long silence of one half of the world', taken from
Elizabeth Robins's speech to the WWSL (Women Writers'
Suffrage League), 1907, sums up the weight of that long silence.

Jaya starts this journey to a consciousness of her self as a
person, the journey to end years of silence, as she enters the

Dadar flat. Significantly, the flat is bare of furniture and the conundrum of housekeeping duties.

The notion of rejecting property and possession is linked to the conversation of Yajnavalkya and Maitreyi on the absolute self in the Fourth Brahmana in the Brahad-aranyaka Upanishad. Maitreyi rejects wealth because it will not give her immortality. The rejection of possession is foregrounded against the folktale of the sparrow who ruthlessly guards her house. Jaya quotes both myth and folktale to understand possessions.

It seems as if her identity as a woman, a wife and mother had been linked only to the acquisition and caring for possessions and the house. Deprived of a house with artefacts, and without the children, Jaya loses the one identity she had constructed to please and to conform to the notion of wife and mother. 'My own career as a wife was in jeopardy. The woman who had shopped and cooked, cleaned, organized and cared for her home and her family with such passion . . . where had she gone? We seemed to be left with nothing but our bodies, and after we had dealt with them we faced blankness . . . nothingness'. (LS 25) With this 'clean slate' and freedom Jaya tries to find her real self, difficult and bewildering because 'ten different mirrors show you ten different faces' (LS 1). These are not 'things told to us by others', and unlike Saru's quest in *The Dark Holds No Terrors* whereby she has to contend with guilt created by the 'other', Jaya's ruminations deal entirely with the self constructed by herself. As Deshpande says, it is Jaya's voice, there is no other perspective.

On entering the flat, the environs replete with memories of Kusum, Jaya comes to an understanding of how she had defined herself as not-Kusum. Kusum was one 'mirror' to show Jaya what she was not – Kusum was a 'poor, frightened, defeated woman, whose urge for destruction had turned inwards' (LS 20). She was distantly related to Jaya but had elicited Jaya's sympathy, understanding and care so that it was Jaya who took charge of her in her madness, housed her in the Dadar flat and felt responsible for her. Jaya feels capable because Kusum is not, empowered because she takes charge of her, sane because Kusum was mad. 'Thank God, Kusum, you're nuts, I had thought; because you're that, I know I'm balanced, normal and sane . . . as long as Kusum was there, I had known clearly who I was; it had been Kusum who had shown me out to be who I was. I was not-Kusum' (*LS* 24). The portrayal of Kusum as a woman rejected by her husband and his family, unwanted by her own family, 'of no use' to anyone, is etched sharply in Jaya's consciousness. The need for women to create a role for themselves and to approximate to a definition of that image is depicted in the picture of the women of Mohan's family. Jaya observes how these women make a career of housekeeping and make themselves integral to the mechanics of daily existence. It is a 'sharply defined role' (Saru had observed that men go to work and women keep the house) and gave to women a sense of self and power. Kamat calls them 'looking-after-others, caring for others women' (*LS* 152). These women are another mirror for Jaya as she considers them to be role models to pattern her self after. There is then a 'consciousness of doing right, freedom from guilt' (*LS* 84).

At the other end of the spectrum is the image propagated by women's magazines, edicts and advice geared towards 'pleasing the man', platitudes that Jaya adopts conscientiously. 'Don't let yourself go. How to keep your husband in love with you. Keep romance alive in a marriage' (*LS* 96).[8] The novel is set in metropolitan Bombay, in the 1970s, foregrounding the conflicts the modern Indian woman would experience in trying to find a balance between the traditional roles performed by women in Mohan's family and the roles propagated by women's magazines. This contradiction is evident in Mohan's *need* for an 'educated, cultured wife', a wife who cuts her hair short 'like Mehra's wife' and wears a housecoat 'like the MD's daughter'. Jaya so conforms to this mirror/look Mohan needs as a validation of his success that when she distances herself to see her self, she sees 'a woman in a crisp cotton sari, with huge dark glasses, shaped eyebrows and short hair . . . I was so exactly like the others, I was almost invisible' (*LS* 142). And yet the image belies what Mohan expects Jaya to be. He re-christens her, in a way re-moulding her: Jaya, meaning victory, named by her father to be different from the other girls who were training to be wives and mothers, victorious because she would go to Oxford, is named Suhasini after marriage.[9] Not only does she 'see' a concept of wifehood that she feels she must follow, what she calls 'the burden of wifehood' (*LS* 121), but she is told stories by Mohan of the silence and repression of his mother in the face of verbal and physical abuse. The dead weight of traditional patterns of wifehood only substantiates the sacrificial actions of women in myth and legend. Sita had unquestioningly followed Rama in exile, Savitri had followed Yama, the god of death, to reclaim her husband Satyavan, and Draupadi had accompanied her five Pandava husbands. Jaya, now symbolically Suhasini, 'a soft, smiling, placid, motherly woman . . . who lovingly nurtured her family . . . a woman who coped' (*LS* 16), follows Mohan to the bare flat. Deshpande says, 'Myths form a large part of this baggage we bring to our self image. How we see ourselves . . . depends greatly on myths . . . a Draupadi or a Savitri . . . are as real as the people around us'.[10] But it is Jaya's perspective that is significant; even while conforming, Jaya can see the wisdom of adopting the strategy of silence.

> He saw strength in the woman sitting silently in front of the fire, but I saw despair. I saw a despair so great that it would not voice itself. I saw a struggle so bitter that silence was the only weapon. Silence and surrender. (*LS* 36)

Deshpande had defined silence as both the oppressor's infliction and a woman's strategy, as indeed it is for the women Jaya 'hears' around the Dadar flat – she hears a man shouting and the sound of blows. 'Tell me. Open your mouth and speak the truth . . . can't you reply? . . . Tell me quick or I'll give it to you' (*LS* 57). Jaya hears moans and sobs but never any reply, only silence. Jeeja, the domestic help, is a silent, dour woman, a battered wife who 'seemed to have no anger behind her silence' (*LS* 51). Vimla does not speak to anybody about her ovarian tumour, and dies, 'her silence intact' (*LS* 39).[11] Mohan's mother and sister are linked by a common destiny, 'the silence in which they died' (*LS* 39). Ritu Menon examines the silences of Saru in *The Dark Holds No Terrors*, Jaya in *That Long Silence*, Kalyani and Sumi in *A Matter of Time* as a single most powerful recurring metaphor in Deshpande's novels. She says that the reason why the women in *A Matter of Time* are self-sufficient is because 'it is a family of *women* living in their *natal* home. There is no one to silence them'.[12]

The community of women, from legend or the neighbour-hood, from Mohan's family or Jaya's, women's magazines or Mohan's dreams, all hold up 'ten different mirrors'. The principle, however, is the same: the husband is a sheltering tree and the woman must be an ideal wife, 'fit' and 'cut' her intellect to please the man. Jaya almost sounds self-congratulatory when she says, 'If Gandhari, who bandaged her eyes to become blind like her husband, could be called an ideal wife, I was an ideal wife too. I bandaged my eyes tightly. I didn't want to know anything' (*LS* 61).[13]

If Jaya thinks she is successful in her similarity to a long line of mythic and literary women in her devotion to her husband, she feels that she is inadequate to the mirror of motherhood as defined by myth, literature and tradition. 'Parents loved their children and children loved their parents' (*LS* 78), Mohan's simple formula does not contain the specific role and expectations of motherhood. Deshpande speaks from personal experience on this issue negating the myths propounded by folk and oral literature.

> The mother myth is of course the most powerful one. The image of the always loving, ever forgiving, sacrificing mother is one that is hard to overcome even today ... When I became a mother I found such a discrepancy between what I was told about mothers and how I felt that it deeply disturbed me. It was only as a writer that I could get past this discrepancy and approached the reality. And I realized that motherhood does not turn you overnight into a different, a nobler, stronger and more loving and loveable individual. You're still the same person you were.[14]

Jaya is disturbed by her response to her children Rati and Rahul. She sounds almost like a spokesperson for Deshpande, replicating the writer's thoughts, substantiating the writer's exploration of the mother's role.

> Whatever had given me the damn fool idea that once I became a mother I would know my children through and through, instinctively? Yes, this is what they had told me: you become a mother, and everything follows naturally and inevitably – love, wisdom, understanding and nobility. (*LS* 173)

Jaya's inability to understand Rahul's actions when he runs away – 'You don't understand, you don't understand anything' (*LS* 131) – or Rati's maturity, are seen by her as her failure. 'A mother? Despairingly I relinquished my halo' (*LS* 173). The novel depicts patterns of motherhood that Jaya cannot relate to – the inadequate Kusum wanting/needing her children, her paternal grandmother, ajji, clinging to her youngest son, the childless Jeeja adopting her husband's son by his second wife, Vanitamami's endless pujas and fasts to have children, and Nayana's numerous pregnancies to have a son. The discussion on motherhood by Urmi and Vanaa in *The Binding Vine* similarly focuses on the 'they' who make motherhood seem so mystical and emotional when the truth is that it's all just a myth (*BV* 76). There is an added dimension to this notion of motherhood when Jaya literally mothers the vulnerable, insecure Mohan. 'I don't like your going away, I don't like being alone here, without you. I feel lost' (*LS* 85).

Thus, the crisis in Mohan's career and the simple Dadar flat brings home to Jaya her distance from the image of wifehood and motherhood that had been created by centuries of tradition, myth and contemporary practice and which she had tried to live up to. Mohan had been, as she says, 'my profession, my career, my means of livelihood'; she had been 'Mohan's wife. Rahul's and Rati's mother. Not myself' (*LS* 173). This definitive fact, baldly stated, occurs to her on reading her writings. Past and present coalesce – Deshpande's recurring narrative technique – and Jaya can 'read' two selves, or see her self from a distance. While in *The Dark Holds No Terrors* Saru had come to her understanding when talking about her turmoil, Jaya in *That Long Silence* comes to it through her writing. 'What we want to reach at finally is the telling. Like in *That Long Silence*. The breaking of silence', says Deshpande.[15] The self-realization occurs within the domestic sphere in the Dadar flat through the most innocuous writings – Jaya's diaries. What she terms 'The Diaries of a Sane Housewife', the painstaking entries of items bought, price lists, dates of children's schools and insurance payments, highlight Jaya's career as a wife and mother. The record of what is written reflects the leitmotiv of Jaya's life, her existence 'cut' to 'fit' a role; what is left out is the person Jaya is, the being who is 'myself' outside these roles. Significantly, Mira in *The Binding Vine* is able to expess her deepest feelings in a diary, but Mira is a poet, writing her diary and poetry simultaneously. The question is whether Jaya is nothing else, or whether the writings reflect the restrained and controlled being she has become while enacting her roles. The beginning of this chapter dealt with these concerns of Deshpande as a woman writer, 'the struggle not to reveal oneself in one's writing' or to see one's writing as self-revelation.[16]

The persona created by Jaya in her short stories and articles: 'plump, good humoured, pea brained but shrewd, devious, skimming over life' (LS 149), Seeta is a mirror to Jaya who lives in the pages of her diary as wife and mother. The easily recognizable traits in the travails of a middle-class bourgeois housewife make her acceptable to Mohan, the editors and the readers. Jaya as seen in her diaries is Seeta, secure and comfortable, unassailable because they both conform, are unquestioning, without anger, restrained and silenced. This stereotypical character is acceptable, the writer/creator is engaged in a 'respectable hobby' (LS 119), contributing to women's magazines, the middles and the weekly columns. Mohan takes credit for allowing his wife the freedom to explore her creativity and is self-congratulatory about being called 'Mr Seeta', till the stories reach beyond the barrier established by him. The intrinsic, literary value of Jaya's writings is unimportant – writings that are within boundaries and do not emanate from personal experience are acceptable. The core of *That Long Silence* is the theme of writing as restraint or self-revelation. The strategy of 'telling' is, however, not acceptable, and stories written not under pseudonyms, stories written without restraint are rejected or recommended to be sent to women's magazines. The first step towards self-realization is Jaya's rejection of Seeta when she stops writing about her. The 'death' of Seeta is also the death of Suhasini, and Jaya casts around for her identity.

Deshpande creates the character of Kamat whose significance in the novel is mainly to reassure Jaya about a self which can be expressed in writing, 'a personal view, a personal vision' that is significant. 'I'll tell you what's really wrong with your story. It's too restrained' (LS 147). He not only provides a sounding board for Jaya, but sees her as a being outside the role she performs. 'With this man I had not been a woman. I had been just myself – Jaya' (*LS* 153). Being herself annihilates Mohan, who sees her only as a wife with the specific characteristics of wifehood. Kamat's role is only to hold up a mirror to Jaya as a self and to the kind of writing she should be expressing that self in. Deshpande, the writer, warns against 'uncontrolled outpourings'. 'Writing is a kind of self revelation ... there is, however, the fear of making my thoughts public. It's like the fear of drinking too much. You might lose control, you might lose your inhibitions. In writing, the sense of control is very important to me. I don't ever intend to let go of it'.[17] Kamat acts as a foil to Jaya: Deshpande has a specific role in mind for her male characters in *That Long Silence*. Both Mohan and Kamat, foils to each other as well, hold up mirrors for Jaya to emulate. Deshpande on being asked about Kamat admits, 'Kamat for me is a part of Jaya. We are brainwashed into believing that the intellectual part is the male part and it's so stupid. ... [I] managed to make Jaya see that she had it in her as well'.[18]. The point that Kamat exists in the novel only in the context of Jaya's self-realization is made with Kamat's death. His death, Deshpande says, 'brings a whole process of defining [Jaya] to a decisive point. If the relationship had gone on, this point of realization would never have come'.[19] For Deshpande, 'women are centre-stage' and Kamat's purpose is served when Jaya understands the worth of writing.

Writing is a serious business, not just a hobby, and Jaya when writing about Seeta never acknowledges that she is a writer. 'No, I'm not really a writer. I just write a bit here and there ... I am not a writer' (*LS* 150). Deshpande notices this sense of self-abnegation in women who come up to her asking her to look at their stories, saying, 'Ha Ha, it's only a hobby. It's nothing serious. I do a little in my spare time'.[20] Self-realization is linked to writing just as Saru's is linked to telling. Jaya's decision by the end of the novel to write is a validation of her discovery of her self. The writing may be like 'a multicoloured patchwork quilt ... a crazy conglomerate of shapes, sizes and colours put together' (*LS* 188) but with this writing she is able to assess herself. 'I've achieved this. I am not afraid anymore. The panic has gone' (*LS* 191). Deshpande has also spoken of her writing as a patchwork quilt – 'In *That Long Silence* I have spoken of Jaya's writing as a patchwork quilt. That is exactly how I think my writing is. I have all these bits and pieces and I have to fit them together'.[21]

Jaya's discovery of her self takes place within the structure of marriage, family and home. Deshpande's women characters do not reach their true self on stepping across the threshold. She is very clear that she is not a chronicler of domestic woes and that self-realization comes within the home. 'What is self-realization but an understanding of the restrictions and regulations you live under? ... I think for the woman understanding her world would begin with the domestic sphere ... what Jaya is feeling stifled by is patriarchal society, the kind of relationship she has with her husband, her role as wife and mother – all exercising power and authority over her.'[22]

Once Jaya realizes that she can go beyond those restrictions and regulations even while living within them but not restrained by them, the understanding, like 'drinking Asterix's magic potion', comes. She can blame neither Mohan nor her set of circumstances. Realization is the first step towards the goal of happiness. She realizes that she had 'cut off the bits ... that had refused to be Mohan's wife. Now I know that kind of fragmentation is not possible. The child ... has been with me through the years. She is with me still' (*LS* 191). Critics have commented on the too easy resolution Jaya arrives at. However, the epigraph of *The Dark Holds No Terrors*, 'you are your own refuge', is illuminating, as Jaya, like Saru, realizes that the onus of creating a self resides only in her self. She quotes Krishna's advice to Arjuna at the end of the Bhagvad-Gita, 'Do as you desire. I have given you knowledge. Now you make the choice. The choice is yours' (*LS* 192). The translation from the closing verse of the Bhagvad-Gita significantly occurs at the closing of the novel. 'Having reflected upon it fully you now act as you choose. Krishna ultimately leaves the decision to act, the will to live the higher life to Arjuna's own choice and independent decision.'[23] Saru and Jaya after reflection have to make possible their conception of themselves, the discovery and knowledge that comes to them after 'telling', and after erasing that long silence. 'I will have to speak, to listen, I will have to erase the silence between us' (*LS* 192). The self has immense possibilities and the power to resist one-dimensional definitions. As Saru awaits Manohar, so Jaya at the end of *That Long Silence* waits for Mohan's return.

The novel, thus, written in the first person, is the story of Jaya – all the characters in the novel have a significance primarily in relation to her. Her lack of communication with her mother, Ai, does not trouble her as Saru's lack of relationship with her mother had. Even the events of the present or the dynamics of her everyday life in the Dadar flat – the domestic crisis in Jeeja's house when the drunk Rajaram is taken to hospital – only enforce the notion of the drama enacted within the four walls of her flat. Ravi running away from a holiday with friends or Mohan leaving her alone only provide occasions for Jaya's reflections on wifehood and motherhood. *That Long Silence* is the one novel of Deshpande's to privilege first-person narration and an interior conversation with the self. Her latest collection of short stories, published earlier but collated under the title *The Stone Women*, highlight the monologue – women from myth and legend are given a voice, a forum for self-expression and the occasion to speak, to 'tell'. The titles of collections of short stories and poems by Indian women writers in English or in translation from regional languages is interesting – *In Their Own Voice* and *The Inner Courtyard*, the titles of some works in English being 'I'm Telling You, Listen' (Hamsa Wadkar, Marathi, 1959), 'Eve Speaks to God' (Kabita Sinha, Bengali, 1976), 'In Search of Myself' (Chhaya Datar, Marathi, 1976), 'My Stricken Voice' (Nidumanuri Revati Devi, Telegu, 1981), and in recent times Anjana Appachana's *Listening Now*. Such titles express the need for women to 'tell', 'speak' and write. The creativity of women writers may be limited to specific areas. Telegu writer Abburi Chhaya Devi, on being asked why she had not written novels, said, 'one can think of plots for stories on the way to the office or sitting on a bus or even while cooking . . . to write a novel you need a lot of time'. Anupama Niranjana says it is difficult for women to collect information and material and they end up dealing with themes that centre on the family.[24] Deshpande telling her own story knits the turmoil of a woman with the idea of retelling, relating and writing. This theme of creativity and of the literary outlet of a woman is elaborated in *The Binding Vine*, Sumi's writing in *A Matter of Time*, and finds its full expression in *Small Remedies*.

With the writing of *That Long Silence* Deshpande felt that she had ended a certain phase in her writing career. In *Roots and Shadows, The Dark Holds No Terrors* and *That Long Silence* she had expressed a point of view and an interiority. She was now ready to move to other themes. 'My book *That Long Silence* was the hardest, the most disjointed, most internalized, most claustrophobic book I had to write ... [it was] my most satisfactory work because I was able to get so much out of my system ... and having got it out of me, I could move on in a way I had not been able to do until then'.[25]

Contemporary reviews seemed to focus on the fact that this was the first of Deshpande's novels to be published outside India, by Virago, a British feminist press. This inaugurated a discussion on the accessibility of the text to the foreign reader. While to Adele King the novel suggested the 'divergences between the worlds of Indian and western women [and] ... how being a woman [was] both similar and different from one society to another',[26] Vrinda Nabar, the author of *Caste as Woman*, warned against such readings. 'It is to be expected, therefore, that a fair number of critics would respond to [the novel] through feminist-tinted glass. This can have its limitations ... a foreign critic of feminist studies referred to *That Long Silence* as an example of how personal life and politics were linked together in contemporary feminist literature', writes Nabar, and goes on to relate what to her is a misreading through the loose application of western feminist theory to the novel.[27] Maria Couto in the *Times Literary Supplement* in fact praises 'this new voice in Britain [who] makes no attempt to explain her culture to a western readership ... Hers is not the India of the ''Raj to Rajiv'' variety'.[28] Deshpande, when asked specifically about publishing this novel with a foreign publisher, avers, 'My novels are not slanted towards a western readership', though she admits that being published abroad made a huge difference to her career. The issue of Indian writing in English published outside India vis-à-vis IWE (Indian writing in English) published in India, or literature in Indian languages, has since acquired the dimensions of a debate, centring primarily on the response of the reader: is the writing aimed at a reader outside India? Is the writing directed in a specific way to 'present' and 'explain' India? Deshpande in the last two decades has written prolifically on these debates, one of her articles significantly titled 'Dear Reader'.[29] With specific reference to *That Long Silence*, Deshpande states that her readership was in India and that this allowed her the space and freedom to write without having to explain certain social cultural practices (like arranged marriages) or myths and legends. 'Here [in India] I will not be slotted as a stereotype of Asian woman. The problem, as I see it, is that the reader who does not happen to be Asian or a woman will think that this novel has nothing to say to him or her'.[30] Shama Futehally, in her review of *That Long Silence* titled 'Of That Elusive Self', expresses the same idea differently. She sees Jaya's attempt to define an elusive self as typifying the quest of the contemporary modern Indian women: 'She has to keep defining and clinging to a place which is somewhere between the grandmother in her village home, the partly Westernized mother in her stainless steel kitchen, the nouveau-riche neighbour with her VCR, the boss's wife who has nothing in her home which isn't foreign, the academic woman marked by her ethnic durries and mirror-work jhola ... and since we have something of all these women in us ... every item which touches our lives becomes invested with a kind of absurd symbolism. A table mat made of plastic and another one of chattai become respectively two kinds of badge ... it is a defining of our own particular pin-point in a conflicting culture web'.[31]

'Our own particular pin-point' is the key phrase in our reading of *That Long Silence*. Deshpande places the consciousness of a woman's identity within her specific social and cultural context, in the 'conflicting culture web' of an everevolving nation. Deshpande says, 'I think my writing has found its place because of feminism. Why would anybody take *That Long Silence* seriously. It's just about a woman who talks about her life and there's not much in it anyway. Whatever it has to say about women's lives has been highlighted because of a feminism'.[32] Later she was to identify *That Long Silence* as 'a loud shriek of despair' before she moved to novels that had 'less stridency, less anger and less confusion'.[33]

48

4

The Binding Vine

Literature is a means of speaking to a reader. *One* reader. It is a private one to one relationship between the author and the reader, between the speaker and the listener, between the voice and the ear. It is not a public oration.

But what *does* a reader want? A sharing of an experience, a world, an idea.[1]

'I hadn't yet completed *That Long Silence* when a casual remark by a friend sparked off what I felt was going to be my next novel. Once *That Long Silence* was off my hands, I opened the doors for this one ... I read an article about euthanasia. Immediately, a young girl, who must have been lurking in my subconscious surfaced: a nurse in the hospital my husband had been working in, who had been raped, brutally injured, and was brain-damaged but did not die, would not die. Over the next few days, she became someone else, distinct from the nurse, and began acquiring a name, a face and a history. The earlier idea and characters gracefully withdrew to give her place. So this young woman was going to be what my next novel was about? But, no! She refused to occupy the centre stage. In fact, characters and events rushed in, but the story had no focus. It took me over a year to realize but there was no single focus here. There were three strands I had to weave into one plait. And so *The Binding Vine*, which is about life and living, about love and possession, about death and ... no, this is cheating. Isn't all literature ultimately about these things? ... the novel is also about controlling women's minds and bodies. But it's really about love.'[2]

Deshpande refuses to define the one core theme of the novel or its single focus. The novel is about all that she says it is, and

49

so much more. If *That Long Silence* could be viewed as a novel about the necessity of writing and *The Dark Holds No Terrors* about verbalizing and the sexual domination of women's bodies, then *The Binding Vine* may be seen as a novel that collates the themes of the previous works in a broader, more intense canvas. Deshpande mentions that, having dealt with the theme in *The Dark Holds No Terrors*, she wished to pursue again the notion of the sexual domination of women's bodies, the idea of a man possessing a woman and claiming monopoly over her body. *The Binding Vine* may also be seen as a novel dealing with the recovery of women's writing (see chapter 1) and the reconstruction of women's lives through writing. Furthering the theme of *That Long Silence*, Lakshmi Holmström says *The Binding Vine* is not only about the silences of women's lives but the silences they sometimes break and the stories they choose to tell. 'In this way [the novel is] fiction, that is, about fiction, and particularly women's fiction.'[3] The novel is also, in Deshpande's words, 'to a large extent, a novel about mothers and daughters'.[4]

Urmila, a lecturer in a college, is, like most of Deshpande's women protagonists, a middle-class professional woman living in Bombay. The novel starts with Urmila grieving over the death of her infant daughter Anu. The notion of loss is a significant recurring theme in Deshpande's works (Dhruva's death in *The Dark Holds No Terrors*, Madhav, the unknown brother lost in *A Matter of Time* and Aditya's death in *Small Remedies*). Deshpande's novels usually start at a point of crisis, which initiates a process of self-discovery for the protagonists. Urmila starts to contend with her loss, with unanswered questions of the past, and an analysis of herself and her marriage to Kishore, after two significant events – the discovery of her mother-in-law Mira's poems, and her involvement with Shakutai, whose daughter Kalpana had been brutally raped. Deshpande's technique of counterpointing the past with the present becomes an axis for Urmila's journey to self-discovery.

Significantly, a trunk of Mira's papers is given to Urmila with the same kind of formality and solemnity that accompanies the handing over of the family jewels to a daughter-in-law in a traditional Indian family. Also significantly, the private papers are handed over by Akka, Kishore's foster-mother, who had been married to Mira's bereaved husband. Akka had been told that the man she was marrying was obsessed with his first wife, Mira, and that 'what he really wanted [now was] a mother for that motherless child' (*BV* 47).[5] Foregrounded against Mira's story, then, is the story of the enormous cruelty of the situation, the fortitude of Akka and her inexplicable and uncharacteristic weeping for Mira. What follows is the recovery and reconstruction of a life, which impinges strangely on Urmi's consciousness and motivates her pursuit of the story of a woman she sees not as Kishore's mother, but as Mira.

Urmila's first-person narrative of Mira's poems turns out to be a discussion on literature, on women's writing, and a historical account of a woman's life, which, through the narrator's vision, acquires a significance for her. Urmila, like Madhu in *Small Remedies*, appears to be almost a spokesperson for writers like Deshpande and editors/translators like Susie Tharu and K. Lalita who have given a voice to or have recovered the writings of women in myth and history. She is initially reluctant to probe into Mira's private papers, 'to trespass, to violate her privacy, to lay bare her tragic story' (*BV* 51). The reader/Urmila is like a voyeur looking into private documents and papers, diaries and poems – forums for self-expression that Jaya, Sumi and Madhu realized were so important for self-definition. 'I have been imagining myself the hunter and Mira my prey; I have been filled with the excitement of the hunter each time I approached her' (*BV* 135). Significantly, Urmi is a woman 'reading' a woman's life: Deshpande, in many instances, has written about the recon-struction, and thereby the biases, of women's lives by men. 'The point is that all these stories in myths, legends and oral literatures have been created by men to fulfill their various needs ... Sometimes it seems to me that words and ideas cannot mean the same to us as they do to men, because what they are really built around is the self-interest of men. Women, let us remember, have not participated in the process of word-making.'[6]

However, Urmi bristles at Priti's suggestions of providing a 'woman's vision' to Mira's life and poems, and is uncomfortable with the thought of an academic dissection and slotting of women's writing. 'And then [Priti] went on to the line of how we had to know our mothers and grandmothers to know our situations. And now, I thought, she will quote Virginia Woolf to me. She did. And I knew then I could not work with her' (*BV* 40).[7] Urmila needs to discover the import of Mira's writings in her specific circumstances, not as an academic exercise geared towards a feminist issue. As Urmi says, 'she's not a symbol, she's Mira who wrote This book is mine as all can tell, if you steal it you will go to hell, the girl who wrote ''Strictly private and confidential'' on her book' (*BV* 40).

Urmi arranges the papers with the same meticulousness with which Mira had arranged hers: 'I've smoothed the scraps of paper, put the notebooks in chronological order, piled the other books together and dusted the ancient file', in a manner similar to Mira's 'workmanlike orderliness about her file of poems' (*BV* 50). Moreover, since 'the past is always clearer because it is more comprehended . . . we can grasp it as a whole' (*BV* 121). Urmila finds it easier to reconstruct it than to cope with the present, 'maddeningly chaotic and unclear' and elusive. Once the papers are organized the question of perspective emerges. How does the researcher present the story? Does she embellish it ('a heroine has to have beauty', *BV* 52)? Does she repress the truth, especially when the recovered story suggests aspects that would hurt Kishore and Vanaa by casting aspersions on their father? Should the recovered stories be published, particularly when in a small town it would implicate Akka ('once people read those poems, how can she hold up her head again?', *BV* 172. Madhu faces a similar dilemma in *Small Remedies*). The question as to why women's stories must be recovered and represented, their silent communion with themselves made public, is bitterly asked by Vanaa: 'It all happened so long ago. Why do you need to rake it up? Why? What do you want?' (*BV* 173).

The story pieced together by Urmi through the diaries written in English and the poems in Kannada ('her thoughts in English, her creative writing in Kannada', *BV* 50; in *Small Remedies* Madhu has to transcribe Bai's interview from Marathi into English) had already been dealt with in 'The Liberated

Woman' and *The Dark Holds No Terrors*.[8] A double perspective on Mira's marriage emerges as Urmi counterpoints Akka's story with the story in Mira's papers: Akka had spoken about her husband's obsession with Mira, his single-minded pursuit of an object, to marry Mira, whom he had 'observed' at a wedding. Urmi notices that the story deals with the perspective of the male 'viewer'. In *A Matter of Time*, Gopal watches Sumi in much the same way that Dushyanta had 'observed' Shakuntala and fallen in love with her in Kalidasa's play *Shakuntala*. Deshpande also refers to the male director's 'gaze' that constructed and depicted Indian movie actress Waheeda Rehman in a way a woman may not have. But there is no testimony to Mira's feeling: 'There's no clue as to what she felt and did. Was she pleased . . . triumphant . . . angry. Did she protest, say anything to her parents?' (*BV* 64). Mira's perspective on this relationship is only 'voiced' in her writings and never becomes a part of an oral family history recounted through succeeding generations. The silence of women's histories is a theme Deshpande explores also in her later novels *A Matter of Time* and *Small Remedies*. In a diary entry, so different from Jaya's in *That Long Silence*, Urmi reads Mira's conversation with her husband, a man insistent and compelling: 'Talk, he says to me, why don't you say something, why don't you speak to me? What shall I talk about, I ask him stupidly . . . and so he goes on, dragging my day, my whole self out of me . . . if this is love it is a terrible thing. What is it he wants from me? . . . why can't he leave me alone' (*BV* 67). Urmi is made aware that Mira's husband tried to 'possess another human being against her will' (*BV* 83). 'It was through all her writing – a strong, clear thread of an intense dislike of the sexual act with her husband, a physical repulsion from the man she married . . . did it have its genesis . . . during their first night together?' (*BV* 63). Mira's aversion to her husband is at odds with the age-old tradition of *Pativrata dharma* (worship of the husband) instilled and internalized in women through myth, story telling, religious indoctrination and exemplum. Even women's autobiographies, Rashundari Debi's *Amar Jiban* (My Life, 1868) and Krupabai Sattianadan's *Saguna* (1895), while dealing with the tribulations of a woman's life did not deal with the transgression of the notion of *Pativrata dharma*. The advice to obey is handed down the ages from mother to daughter. Mira writes

> Don't tread paths barred to you
> obey, never utter a 'no';
> submit and your life will be
> a paradise, she said and blessed me

> (*BV* 83)

The appropriation of women's bodies and minds is initiated at the time of marriage with the change in name; the survival of past traditions in today's India is made plain when we see Jaya, in *That Long Silence*, renamed. Mira is rechristened Nirmala, the name even Urmi had known her by before she discovered her as Mira.

> Who is this? None but I,
> my name hence, bestowed upon me.
> Nirmala, they call, I stand statue-still.
> Do you build the new without razing the old?
> A tablet of rice, a pencil of gold
> can they make me Nirmala? I am Mira.

While appearing to submit, Mira reflects a spark of independent thinking: 'I have learnt to say "no" at last' (*BV* 67), or the assertive 'I am Mira'. Mira uses her writing to subvert traditional myths and rewrite them from a women's perspective. Evoking the myth of the divine couple Laxmi Narayanan – to which, Deshpande explains, a newly wed couple is often compared – Mira writes about the apprehension of Laxmi. Did she tremble, 'fearing the coming of the dark clouded, engulfing night?' (*BV* 66). Explaining the irony of this myth in the context of Mira's life, Deshpande says, 'But to Mira, who has to live with a husband she does not love, has to submit unwillingly to sex with him almost every night of her life, the image is transformed into something different.' Deshpande hopes for women writers to be able to reinterpret myths and write from the woman's point of view. 'What women writers are doing today is not a rejection of the myths but a meaningful and creative reinterpretation of them.'[9] Like Urmi, Jaya, Sumi and Madhu, Mira is a woman writer who writes her life and reworks in her writings myths aimed at conditioning women.

Urmi surmises that it was only her writing that had kept Mira going while she was cloistered at home, living with a man she did not love, without a space, a room of one's own. She would have written stealthily, like Rashundari Debi, at night. Urmi precedes Madhu in *Small Remedies* who looks for meaning in writing Bai's life: both Urmi and Madhu, contending with the loss of a son and daughter respectively, see their writing and the subject of their writing – Mira the poet and Bai the singer – as a means of recovery. Urmi understands a meaning in Mira's writings that has a personal significance for her. 'But what does the reader want?', Deshpande had asked, 'a sharing – of an experience, a world, an idea'.[10]

The answer is given partially in Mira's story, strangely related to the story of Shakutai's daughter, Kalpana, the link made by the narrator Urmi, who reads in the past a meaning for the present. The germ of the story of *The Binding Vine*, which refused to be 'centre-stage' for Deshpande but was the starting point, one of the three strands of the plait, the brutal rape of a young girl, finds expression in Kalpana's story. On a visit to Vanna, working in a hospital, Urmi encounters the hysterical, distraught mother of the rape victim. Shakutai's insistent cry in the hospital contains the paranoid fear of social stigma and of aspersions on her daughter's reputation: 'my daughter is not that kind of a girl . . . you people are trying to blacken my daughter's name . . . I'll never be able to hold up my head again, who'll marry the girl, we're decent people' (*BV* 58). Deshpande deals with truth vis-à-vis reportage, with public knowledge vis-à-vis silence in women's lives and writings. The silences that surround women's lives and the silences they surround themselves with are a recurring thread in her works, from *The Dark Holds No Terrors* and *That Long Silence* to *A Matter of Time* and *Small Remedies*. In *The Binding Vine*, Shakutai demands a silence, a repression of the truth to safeguard her daughter's reputation (later, in *Small Remedies*, Deshpande was to look into the enormous gaps in Bai's life that Bai refused to fill in for her). The fear of public opprobrium is more terrifying to Kalpana's mother than the desire to find the culprit and punish him. The truth must be hidden, to protect the victim and her family, especially the younger sister of marriageable age. The police are complicit with

Shakutai's insistence to repress the truth because rape cases are 'messy and troublesome, never straightforward' (*BV* 88). Moreover, the police believe that the girl may have invited this kind of attention: 'for all you know she may be a professional . . . she must have been out with a boyfriend' (*BV* 88). For both the mother, Kalpana's guardian, and the police, the official guardians of law, the verdict is the same – Kalpana's rape is not to be recorded. Moreover, Kalpana had displayed an independence and wilfulness which transgressed the boundaries of that society. 'Cover yourself decently, I kept telling her, men are like animals. But she went her way. You should have seen her walking out, head in the air, caring for nobody. It's all her fault . . . all her fault' (*BV* 147). The fear that women must have and the constraints they must live within are points driven home repeatedly by Shakutai: 'we have to keep to our places, we can never step out' (*BV* 148). The 'place' is defined by a patriarchal society ever willing to throw stones. Kalpana, however, asserted 'I'm not afraid of anyone', stepped out confidently, and broke the code that kept her confined. The assertion of her self ended in a ghastly assault on her body.

Kalpana's story of rape gives Urmi the insight into Mira's poem and diaries: 'I've suddenly realized – what has happened to Kalpana happened to Mira too' (*BV* 63). Kalpana's rape is the clue that Urmi needs to understand Mira's relationship with an obsessive husband – the theme of marital rape also dealt with in 'The Liberated Woman' and *The Dark Holds No Terrors*. Moreover, Mira's poems, like Kalpana's story, lie hidden.

The paranoia of mothers protecting their daughters from the danger of sexual assault is a significant theme in the novel. Vanaa cautions her daughters, Inni is hysterical when Urmi is late returning home, and Shakutai moans, 'Why does God give us daughters?' (*BV* 150). Mira's poem and Shakutai's concern for her daughters and hopes for her own future become the axis for Urmi's memories of her daughter Anu. The theme of motherhood, dealt with in Deshpande's previous novel, is discussed intensely in *The Binding Vine*. Saru in *The Dark Holds No Terrors* and Jaya in *That Long Silence* felt that they as mothers did not approximate to the myths of glorified motherhood propounded by legend: moreover, as daughters they were closer to their fathers. In *The Binding Vine*, almost for the first time, Deshpande depicts, in Urmi's grief for Anu, the all-absorbing love of motherhood, a theme she takes up in Madhu's obsessive love for her son Aditya in *Small Remedies*. From the memories of physical touch – 'I can feel the softness of her body ... the heaviness of her head' – to every sensory perception – 'I hear the soft snuffling sounds of her breathing ... I can smell her sweet baby's flesh' (*BV* 21) – Urmi is obsessed with her love for her daughter. She is able to relate to Shakutai and her grief: they are both mothers, one having lost her daughter, the other on the verge of losing hers. The connectedness, however, is in the dreams and aspirations that mothers have for their daughters. Shakutai worked to give Kalpana all the things she never had, 'education, a good life, a good marriage, respect from others ... I don't want my children to be like me' (*BV* 112). (Later, in *Small Remedies*, Munni does not wish to be like her mother). Urmi realizes that Inni had dreams for her marriage, for a world for her daughter that was her ideal, 'a pearls and chiffons sort of existence'. Urmi's dream was to let her daughter soar, be unfettered, climb high. Mothers want to give their daughters 'the world [they] dreamt of for [themselves]' (*BV* 124). Mira's poem addressed to her mother, seeing Mira dressed in a green sari and green bangles, signs of marriage and fertility, has a touch of pathos – unspoken in the poem is the mother's desire to see her daughter fulfil a destiny meant for every woman, marriage and children. 'She saw me married, she saw me pregnant and she was happy' (*BV* 126). The pathos lies in the fact that the dream turns sour and the daughter becomes a reflection of the mother – 'unsmiling, grave, bedewed with fear ... Mother, I'm now your shadow' (*BV* 120). Saru in *The Dark Holds No Terrors* inhabits her mother's puja room, looks and acts like her.

The theme of the daughters playing the roles and lives of their mothers is taken up in *A Matter of Time*, while in *Small Remedies* Munni models her self as an antithesis to her mother. Deshpande refers to this aspect in the essay 'The Indian Woman – Myths, Stereotypes and the Reality'. In fact, the theme of this essay is voiced by Urmi in a discussion on motherhood with Vanaa: 'Sometimes, I think, they brainwash us into this motherhood thing. They make it seem so mystical and emotional when the truth is that it's all just a myth. They've told us so often and for so long that once you're a mother, you have these feelings, that we think we do' (*BV* 77). Mrinal Pande, in 'Recollecting Motherhood', says,

> A close reading of women's writings from the Therigatha (The Songs of Buddhist Nuns), to Mahasweta Devi's and Ambai's fiction reveals that motherhood as women truly experienced it and motherhood as a much glorified institution are as separate and distinct from each other, as Gandhiji is from Gandhism. As an institution, motherhood comes to young women, as an already perfected idea, a system built by a patriarchal society. And when the family elders bless them and say 'may you be the mother of many sons', it has all the heaped force of custom and tradition, behind it.[11]

The novel also deals with the very real problems of career women and children resentful of absent mothers. The answer to the mystery of Urmi being adopted by her paternal grandparents lies in the demands and expectations of motherhood by men. Her father thought Inni was incapable of looking after the child Urmi, and on finding Urmi alone with a trusted male servant, punishes Inni by taking Urmi away to his mother. Deshpande quotes the psychoanalyst Sudhir Kakkar who speaks of the 'good mother' picture as being a male construct.[12]

Urmi's self-discovery and her ability to cope with her grief rests on her interaction with two people – Mira and Shakutai. Both survivors, in different contexts, give Urmi the impetus to take charge. She realizes that she had managed the affairs of her life – Baiajji's death, Aju's hanging, marriage to Kishore, who is absent most of the time, and her father's death – with competence because she was lucky. Deshpande says, 'In *The Binding Vine*, Urmi has to go through the whole exercise of understanding the privileges she has had and what she really is without all that. Not only is she privileged to start with, she is also unconscious of her privileges. To her that is existence. Finally, she is able to see and cross the line to those who do not have what she has. But first she must open her eyes and see her self.'[13] Urmi realizes that Mira and Shakutai's voice cannot be silenced and repressed, 'pushed under the carpet', any more for fear of disgrace. Urmi's final realization comes with her decision to publish Mira's poems and to make public the story of Kalpana's rape. An attempt to recover the stories of women or give voice to their lives is fraught with criticism. Urmi's friendship with Vanaa is almost destroyed when the criticism comes forcefully not from outside but from Vanaa, a woman who lives a conventional life and fears her husband (Vanaa starts every sentence with 'Harish says'; Urmi, aware of the implications, says, 'you let him bulldoze you, you crawl before him'). Moreover, the public outcry over Kalpana's rape and the attempt of the authorities to first conceal it and then be dismissive about it generates morchas, demands for an enquiry, and television fame for Kalpana's family. Talking about rape, Deshpande says, 'everybody wants to hush it up . . . I would say Yes, make it public, but when it comes to my own daughter, my own self, would I? Sometimes organizations lack compassion and sensitivity in dealing with these conflicts. In *The Binding Vine* I have tried to represent this situation.'[14]

The public hue and cry results in the identification of the rapist – Kalpana's uncle Prabhakar, who had demanded Kalpana from his childless wife, in exchange for continued protection: the assault on Kalpana was to teach her a lesson for thwarting his advances and daring to dream of marriage with someone else – daring to be independent. Deshpande has spoken about the complicity of women in the power game of dominance – subservience in gender relations. Sulu's attempt to hold on to her marriage impels her to pawn Kalpana. Her silence about Prabhakar's motives is broken only after the story is made public, and with disastrous consequences. Deshpande seems to be asking about the 'wages' of breaking a silence and of telling a story. The recovery of Mira's poems, the story of her repression and the domination of her mind and body would implicate others – Vanaa and Kishore's father and Akka's father. A reputation in a small town, where a friendship between the sexes is frowned upon, would be tarnished (a theme taken up in Bai's life in *Small Remedies*).

Vanaa and Inni view with suspicion even Bhaskar's friendship with Urmi. Bhaskar joins a line of male characters in Deshpande's novels – Madhav and Boozie in *The Dark Holds No Terrors*, Kamat in *That Long Silence* and Chandru in *Small*

Remedies – who are created simply to highlight some aspect of her women protagonists. Deshpande seems to be suggesting that a non-sexual relationship between men and women is not possible. Bhaskar, taking advantage of the absent Kishore, infers that Urmi did not love her husband. Bhaskar's insistence motivates Urmi to analyse her marriage to Kishore, his absence and his loveless passion. As for Bhaskar, he is as easily dismissed under the recognizable safeguard of virtue and chastity – Sita's blade of grass, in the epic *Ramayana*, to thwart Ravana's advances – as Kamat is in *That Long Silence*.

Kishore exists outside the pages of the novel, except in Urmi's consciousness, and is similar to both Manohar in *The Dark Holds No Terrors* and Mohan in *That Long Silence*. Deshpande says, 'Men are in the wings . . . while writing *The Binding Vine* I kept promising to leave all the male characters intact. And they are all gone.'[15]

Deshpande touches on issues of the translation of women's writing from one regional language, Kannada, into English, and on the bilingualism of characters who converse in Marathi and Kannada with ease (both languages spoken in Deshpande's home). Urmi translates Mira's poems, written in Kannada, into English, though she intends to publish them in Kannada. Deshpande appreciates the work done by Susie Tharu and K. Lalita, and by Lakshmi Holmström, in translating a vast compendium of women's writing in regional languages into English. Set against Mira's poems is the advice given to her by the male poet Venu, 'why do you need to write poetry? It is enough for a young woman like you to give birth to children. That is your poetry. Leave the other poetry to us men' (*BV* 127). In fact it is Mira's poem which helps Urmi 'solve the rest of the crossword . . . now, with this poem, Mira has cleared my emotional life, swept away the confusing tangle of cobwebs' (*BV* 137). The poem on the 'cord of this binding vine of love' reiterates the theme of recovery after loss, of life and loving, of love and possession.

The Binding Vine was published first by Virago Press, London, and then by Penguin, India, in 1993. Lakshmi Holmström's review mentions the cover of the Virago edition, based on a reproduction of a portrait by Anjolie Ela Menon, which could be a representation of any of the three women, Urmi,

Mira or Kalpana, whose stories are intertwined in the novel.[16] Adele King's review focuses again, as did her review of *That Long Silence*, on the 'similarities and important differences in the lives of the middle class educated Indian women with women's lives in the West'.[17] Her notion of Mira's arranged marriage is commented on by Deshpande as a western response that misses the point. 'The fact that labels pre-empt meaning is evident in one Western response to Mira's story in *The Binding Vine* which found it to be the story of an arranged marriage. Since most marriages then were arranged, I think an Indian reader would most probably discount that factor. Such preconceptions or expectations limit the range of communication that writers desire. They are also different from cultural particularities which will always exist.'[18] Maria Couto in fact appreciates these very cultural particularities which Deshpande so unselfconsciously writes about. 'She brings to the Indian novel in English a structure of life and society such as informs novels in the Indian languages, introducing the reader to the ambience of lower middle class life in homes without an English veneer and without the hybridity of the urban upper classes.'[19]

The concerns of the novel are best summed up by Deshpande's statement on feminism. The novel is a work about love and recovery. 'Today, when I call my self a feminist, I believe that the female of the species has the same right to be born and survive and to fulfill herself and shape her life according to her needs and the potential that lies within her, as the male has.'[20] Urmi survives the grief of her daughter's death, Kalpana has the resilience of youth, and Mira's voice, recovered by Urmi, will find a place in the literary history of Indian writing.

5

A Matter of Time

> It's hard for women everywhere, and a little harder for
> Indian women because the family really does claim you.
> It's not just the immediate family; it's the extended family,
> and most of the family duties are taken over by women.
> The men are the pillars of the family, but the work,
> including the emotional network and the bonding and all
> these things like bringing the family together – it is all
> done by women. . . .
>
> I am a woman, and I do write about women, and I'm
> going to say it loudly.[1]

'Now, Shashi Deshpande cannot be fixed into any neat
category like a feminist but one can't help noticing that she is
more at ease, and at her best when dealing with women', is the
pronouncement in a review of *A Matter of Time*, Deshpande's
seventh novel, published by Penguin, India, in 1996 and by the
Feminist Press, New York, in 1999.[2] A novel centring on three
generations of women living together in an ancestral home
almost to the near exclusion of men, it marked a new phase in
Deshpande's literary career. *That Long Silence* ended an intro-
spective phase when a lot was suppressed within her and
when she had written *Roots and Shadows* and *The Dark Holds No
Terrors*. She said that she was 'very confident of this book. It
[was] written for [that] stage of my life.'[3] In a conversation with
me, Deshpande said that *A Matter of Time* was her favourite
book because of her deep understanding and closeness to the
characters. As a writer, Deshpande now feels that she had
found her oeuvre, her material:

> More than anything else I had written till then [it] was about the
> world of women, almost claustrophobically so . . . Through the

articulation of a lifetime's experiences, thoughts and introspection, through the lives of the women I had created, I had done something so that I could never see myself or my writing in the same way again.[4]

Deshpande had written till then seven novels, four books for children and almost eighty short stories.[5] But 'Silence condensed everything I wanted to say and after that I moved away from the personal, the internal, to the outward.'[6]

The first discernible change in the shift to the "outward" is the shift in the location of the story of the novel to Bangalore, a city Deshpande with her husband and two sons had shifted to from Bombay some years before. She had, however, continued to set her novels in Bombay, Saptagiri, ancestral villages and small towns. Location is of prime significance in Deshpande's works and the dynamics of the city – Bombay in *That Long Silence* and *Small Remedies*, the small towns and villages in *That Long Silence, The Dark Holds No Terrors* and *Small Remedies* – are pivotal to her works and characters. Deshpande admits that living in Dharwar till she was fourteen made her understand that 'a small town never leaves you'.[7] The locations are a 'matrix from which her characters, particularly her female characters, spring, and they form an essential part of "the kind of people they are ... ordinary people", Deshpande says, "people like you and me going about their daily business." Teachers, lawyers, doctors ... they are modest and unassuming – far removed from the flash of MTV and designer shoes. In a sense, they are the heart of middle India.'[8] The criss-cross of lane and alleys through which Aru rides her scooter, the courtesies of those who escort her when she loses her way, the change of seasons evident in nature – the flowering gulmohar tree and the mango blossoms or the heat, Cubbon Park, the portrayal of the property agent Nagaraj – are typical aspects of Bangalore where Deshpande now lives. The idea of the novel came to her significantly when she saw an old stone house with a garden, a relic of its past glory, in Malleswaran, a locality still exuding an old-world charm in Bangalore, now the computer capital of India. Deshpande says that in her mind she saw the figures of three women going into this house: in this, combined with the real-life experience of a friend's mother who, after forty years of marriage, was abandoned by her husband, she found the story of *A Matter of Time*. Her imagination took her backwards and behind the return of the woman and her three daughters to her natal home.

Significantly, the epigraph to the novel appears below a heading, 'The House', focusing on the significance of house, householder and property. Yajnavalkya, a great sage to whom the sun revealed the *White Yajur Veda*, says to his wife Maitreyi, 'verily I am about to go forth from this state (of householder)'. Taken from the Brhad-aranyaka Upanishad, it refers to the movement towards renunciation.[9] In the third stage of a man's life, the householder decides to leave his house *grahastha* (domestic life) and enter the fourth stage of his life to become the anchorite, *vanaprastha*. (The reference to Yajnavalkya offering his property to Maitreyi in *That Long Silence* is as pivotal to the story of Jaya as this reference is to Gopal.) The epigraph is the point of entry to the section 'The House' and the chapter that follows, but more importantly to the story of Gopal and Shripat, the two male characters in a novel in which three generations of women are 'centre-stage'.

Saru and Jaya at a point of crisis had returned to their natal homes, and now, in *A Matter of Time*, Sumi with her three daughters returns to her natal home: the past counterpoints the present in evoking, in a different set of circumstances, Kalyani's return with her two daughters Sumi and Premi to this house. The Big House, known as Vishwas (trust) contains in its architecture and history the complexities and dynamics of the story and the characters, past and present. Deshpande says,

> For me it's essential – almost as essential as it is for a movie
> director – to have the shape of the house clear. I know all the
> houses in my novels . . . as an architect does, all the rooms, even if
> I may not use them. If I have that clear then the rest of it can
> happen, because it is there that it is going to happen.[10]

The novel starts and ends with a description of the house, a backdrop to the figures of Kalyani and Aru, representing the past and the future, two women signifying the bonds of mother and daughter, representing tradition and modernity

64

and yet continuity. The house, despite its solidity and the *avatar* of strength emanating from its history through generations, and the fact that it provides refuge to the abandoned Kalyani and later to Sumi, does not give to its inmates a sense of nurture. Like the ancestral home in *The Dark Holds No Terrors*, the house reflects the 'schizophrenic' existence of Kalyani and Shripati, with Shripati's solitary room on the floor above – 'the room seems to have taken on ... the personality of the man inhabiting it, so that there is something guarded about it, an air of reserve' (*MT* 71), leaving the living space below entirely to the women.[11] The four generations of women are represented by Kalyani, distanced and ostracized by her husband and often visited by her adopted sister Goda, Sumi her daughter abandoned by Gopal, and Sumi's three daughters Aru, Charu and Seema, all watched over by the stern portrait of Manorama, the tyrannical, dominating and wilful mother of Kalyani. However, the definition of the house now as a zenana suppresses the tensions and oppressions of the unseen, silent presence of Shripati and the mystery behind his renunciation of family life well before the period prescribed by the Upanishad. Gopal, the householder who went away, and Shripati are unseen presences impinging on the consciousness of all the women in the house. (Significantly, both had come to the house before they were married to the daughters of the house – Shripati as the younger, needy brother of Manorama, for ever obliged to his sister for providing him with an education, and Gopal as a tenant, both outsiders, yet attached to the house). The all-women household and its activities also suppress two clues to the mystery of the Kalyani–Shripati relationship and its parallel to the Sumi–Gopal relationship: the imperative of Property Ownership and the need for a male child.

In India the 'existence of separate personal laws based on different religions also affects gender relation ... And all religious laws favour men in matters relating to property rights and inheritance.'[12] The absence of a male heir and the need to retain the Big House impel Manorama to marry her only daughter Kalyani, silenced into submission, to her brother Shripati: 'Manorama wanted a son; instead there was Kalyani ... for Manorama she became the visible symbol of their failure to have a son' (*MT* 150–51). Manorama's fear that Vithalrao would marry again to have a son, together with her love of property, lead her to take Kalyani out of school and marry her to her brother, a practice not unknown in southern India. 'Perhaps after this, Manorama felt secure. The property would remain in the family now. Her family' (*MT* 129).[13] These are not just the fears of a woman conditioned by her times: as a daughter, even Sumi feels alien in the house, despite the reassurance of her father, and admits that one day this house will belong to Nikhil, Premi's son and the only male heir of the family. 'The male child belongs' (*MT* 7). The novel is replete with references to sons – lost or dead – and the resultant lacunas, and, in the songs sung in celebrations of the birth of Nikhil, references abound in the banter revolving around Rohit, Lalita's son and Raghupati's grandson. 'The walls of this house . . . seem to cry out that the very reason for their existence was a son' (*MT* 71). Significantly, at the end of the novel Aru cries out spontaneously when Kalyani collapses at the death of her husband and daughter, 'Amma, I'm here, I'm your daughter, Amma, I'm your son, I'm here with you' (*MT* 233); and again, calmly, 'I'm your daughter, Amma, I'm your son' (*MT* 244). The significance of a son in the religious, cultural, social context of India has endured from ancient times to the present. Throughout the novel, from the Brhad-aranyaka Upanishad quotation – 'whatever wrong has been done by him,/ his son frees him from it all;/ therefore he is called a son. By his/ son a father stands firm in this world' (*MT* 91) – to the epigraph to the 'Family' section, or the statements of Aru, the modern, educated heroine of the novel, 'I'm your son', Deshpande makes central the import of a son. This, even in a text dealing entirely with the stories of Manorama, Kalyani, Sumi and Aru. The impacting of Property, the Son and the Big House is the core of Deshpande's novel (just as writing, telling and speaking were the core of her previous novels), marking a major departure from the interiority and silences of the earlier works.

Resisting the label of someone who writes only about women – 'people seem to think that you are writing about women. I am writing about Jaya; I am writing about Saru . . . and I am writing about Mira. Not *women*[14] – Deshpande makes another major departure from her previous works. The focus of the crisis at the beginning of *A Matter of Time* is not on the retreat of the women protagonists to their natal homes – as it had been for Saru and Jaya, and is now for Sumi. The inner journey, the exploration of an interiority, a single perspective, reflections, discovery and understanding through 'telling' and 'writing' are not the preserve any longer of the women characters. In *A Matter of Time* it is Gopal, Sumi's husband, who leaves his wife and daughters, and, literally 'stripped bare' of the constructs of middle-class existence – his house and job – retreats into a small room devoid of all comforts. While the epigraphs of *The Dark Holds No Terrors* and *That Long Silence* related to Saru and Jaya, the epigraph to *A Matter of Time* is a window to the inexplicable action of Gopal the householder who leaves the world. 'What is it . . . that makes a man in this age of acquisition and possession walk out on his family and all that he owns? . . . how then can you, in this age, a part of this society, turn your back on everything in your life?' (*MT* 27). While talking about the politics of being a woman writer with Mahasweta Devi, Githa Hariharan, C. S. Lakshmi and Pratibha Ray, Deshpande states, 'All these years men have been telling the world in their writing that women, not men, are mysterious, women are fascinating, women are strange . . . so now women are also talking and telling the world that men are strange, men are mysterious . . . so many of their things we don't understand. You may be very close to your friend or husband or lover or whatever but at the same time there's always that element of the unknown.'[15] Gopal is Deshpande's favourite male character and she invests him with sensitivity and a sensibility that can only be termed feminine; Menon notes that she invests him with the qualities usually reserved for her female protagonists – reflection and introspection.[16] Moreover, unlike Mohan in *That Long Silence*, Urmila's husband Kishore in *The Binding Vine* and Manohar in *The Dark Holds No Terrors*, Gopal is given a voice and a perspective – in fact his is the only first-person narration in a novel written in the third person, and this is the first time a male narrator's voice is used in a Deshpande novel. In an interview with Menon, Deshpande says, 'I wanted to see if I could use a male voice again . . . but not as I used to earlier [in her short stories]. It was really something of a challenge.[17] Deshpande's narrative technique explores a double perspective when following every narrative of Kalyani's, Aru's and Sumi's visit to Gopal the focus shifts to Gopal's first-person narrative of the same incident. If Kamat represented the intellectual side of Jaya, Gopal could be said to represent the emotional. He analyses his self, which he feels is defined only by his relationship with his wife and daughters; 'but now I know I had only lost myself in that beautiful, dense green foliage' (*MT* 45). Gopal's reflections sound dangerously close to Saru's and Jaya's, women analysing their identity as wives and mothers. Gopal feels claustrophobic – 'It's not easy to be the only male in a family of females. You feel so . . . shut out' (*MT* 60), lost, alienated from the cocoon of mother and child, 'they belonged together as I never did . . . and I was outside. A man is always an outsider' (*MT* 68). He admits frankly to fear and earns the respect of woman activist lawyer Surekha, as he is able to do 'something most men found hard – present his whole self to a female, not just a part of himself' (*MT* 107). In the characterization of Gopal it seems that Deshpande, with growing mastery over her characters and technique, was exploring the interiority of a male just as she had with the females, Saru, Jaya and Urmi. She admits that this was the first time she was closer to a male character than the female and that she understood Gopal's decision to leave his family even though many had a problem with it. Gopal's reflections, imbued with the philosophies, stories and legends from Indian mythology and religion, seek answers to the meaning of life and self. Unlike Shripati, Gopal's 'absent presence' in the book is a strong force that brings, in turn, Kalyani, Aru, Seema, Sumi and Premi to his 'retreat'. Menon feels that 'Gopal sets the story in motion, and literally speaking, it begins and ends with him . . . he is drawn back into the story in a movement almost parallel to Sumi's moving out of it'.[18]

The complex interplay of relationships and characters, the parallels between past and present, the double perspective – 'life must be lived forwards, but it can only be understood backwards' – is handled to near perfection in *A Matter of Time*, a prelude to the complete mastery of technique in *Small Remedies*. The continuity in the four generations of women,

68

Manorama, Kalyani, Sumi and Aru, who resembles Manorama's mother Arundhati, the seemingly common pattern in the lives of Kalyani and Shripati, on the one hand, and Sumi and Gopal on the other, is never simply stated. Kalyani's past, her troubled relationship with her mother (a throw-back to Saru's with hers in *The Dark Holds No Terrors*), or the mystery of Shripati's coldness for thirty years, her story and frustrations, appear in vignettes. Sumi remembers seeing Kalyani standing before a closed door, banging on it, shrieking wildly and in vain before slumping to the ground (*MT* 74), or again, standing, striking her face with both her hands in a terrifying scene reminiscent of Mohan's mother in *That Long Silence*. Kalyani's past lives on in Sumi; 'it has stained our bones'. It lives on in Sumi's present when she fears that 'what is happening to me now [may] become part of my daughters too? Will I burden them with my past and my mother's as well?' (*MT* 75). It exists in Premi's bald statement to Gopal, 'don't do this to your girls, Gopal' (*MT* 135). And in Sumi's realization, 'it seemed like something being repeated – my mother then, me now. And my daughters? But now I know my life is not like my mother's' (*MT* 222). Shama Futehally and Ritu Menon refer to the theme of silence in *A Matter of Time*. 'Silence, whether forced or voluntary, whether imprisoning or freeing, lasting days or lasting years, has been a recurring theme with Shashi Deshpande, one of those which make her work a united whole.'[19] However, to a greater extent the women in this novel are able to share and express their concerns and anxieties. The areas of silence relate to the men, Shripati and Gopal.

The past, always present however unobtrusively (within Kalyani, within Sumi, in Manorama's portrait), is to be forgotten because the image of Kalyani bustling through the house, organizing beds, clothes, food – 'the mustard seed of domestic life' (*MT* 36) cannot be associated with the 'hysterical, self punishing women' (*MT* 185) Sumi had also pushed away from memory. Deshpande invests all the women characters with an inner strength and resilience that gives them the capacity not only to cope but to 'let go' and move on. From Charu, geared up for her admission to medical college, believing that 'they must get on with their lives' (*MT* 58), to

Sumi, who at a deeper level is the only one to understand Gopal's decision and who states time and again, 'let him go . . . just let him go', because 'I'm not interested [in punishing him]. I just want to get on with my life' (*MT* 61) – they all cope. Even Manorama had displayed strength of mind in attempting to alter her *karma* (fate) and forcing circumstances to suit her agenda, even if it meant sacrificing her daughter's happiness in marrying her to her brother, a man Sumi surmises had a kind of 'suppressed savagery' and who was probably against the marriage. Aru comes close to Manorama in her desire to change the circumstances and to force a meaning out of their tangled life. Her visits to Gopal and her association with the activist lawyer Surekha, her attempts to protect Sumi, and to 'make sense of what is happening, her consciousness moving outside her self and reaching out to the others as well, embracing, in fact, the whole of what is happening' (*MT* 185) give her a pre-eminent role in Deshpande's scheme. Besides continuities and similarities, links are established. Aru, her name similar to that of Arundhati, her great grandmother's mother, looks like Manorama, her great grandmother, and bonds with Kalyani, at the end of the novel becoming both her child and her protector. Kalyani and Sumi are linked not only because they are both, for different reasons abandoned by their husbands – they are both still wives, not widows. The social/religious code accords a privileged status to the wife, who is always superior to the widow, the prostitute and the unmarried.

> It is enough to have a husband, and never mind the fact that he has not looked at your face for years . . . Does this wifehood make up for everything . . . her kumkum is intact and she can move in the company of women with the pride of a wife . . . to have a husband living is everything. But – Oh my God, oh my God!

Deshpande in her body of work examines the myths associated with wifehood and motherhood in various permutations. I see *A Matter of Time* as a novel that examines major issues of Indian society as Deshpande moves away from the interiority of a woman's reflections on these issues to the outer world. Issues of class and caste are reflected in several themes of the novel: the old story of Manorama's marriage to Vithalrao; the education of woman (discussed in chapter 1), spanning the spectrum from the time when Yamunabai was at school to Kalyani's break in education, to Shripati's ambitions to make Sumi a lawyer and Premi a doctor, to Charu filling in her forms for medical school; the import of Property and Inheritance linked to the god-like position accorded to the son (the rates of female foeticide in India are increasing with the availability of sophisticated medical tests to determine the sex of the child); and the counterpointing of tradition and modernity, an issue widely relevant in a nation fast developing into an industrialized, globalized economy, best reflected in a household of three different generations. This is also manifest in the continuity/contrast between Manorama and Aru, both women in charge, able to cope and contend with the vicissitudes of life, both a testimony to the centrality of women, half of the world's people, no longer silenced. Men may be 'the pillars of the family', or they may not, but as Deshpande asserts, 'everything is done by women'.

Significantly, Sumi is seen by Gopal as the mythic Parvati, wife of Siva, 'drawing all the colour and movement . . . into her self . . . filling him with astonishment and delight' (*MT* 45); or as Shakuntala, enchanting him so that he loses himself (the Shakuntala–Dushyanta myth is the axis around which the Sumi–Gopal relationship is discussed). But Sumi is seen by the novelist as calm, capable and efficient. She packs up her home with admirable detachment and returns to the Big House. She moves on without recrimination, looking for an alternative house only to protect her daughters from the bad atmosphere of the strained man–woman relationship evident in the Big House. And when she finds an outlet for her creativity, in writing a play, *The Gardener's Son*, it so impresses that she is offered a job in a school and is ready to leave with Seema and start her life again. The recurring trope of writing as a means of self-expression has been discussed in almost every novel of Deshpande's. For Sumi, the choice of a subject matter is very significant: she wants to write about Surpanakha, the demon sister of Ravana, whose desire for Rama and Lakshmana results in the cutting off of her nose and the Rama–Ravana war in the epic *The Ramayana*. Sumi wants to give Surpanakha a voice and stress her courage in displaying both her sexuality and desire, and her courage in departing from the stereotypical situation in which the man expresses his desire for the woman – Dushyanta watching Shakuntala, for example. In this she is almost a spokesperson for Deshpande, who gave a voice to the Stone Women, women always seen through the male 'gaze'. Deshpande writes about women authors rewriting myths and legends 'in their own voice': Irawati Karve's *Yuganta* ('in her readings I see how differently a woman saw [the characters in the Mahabharata], how much more real, more plausible the women seemed'); Vaidehi's version of Shakuntala, in which Shakuntala exercises her independence and refuses to go back to Dushyanta; K. R. Usha's 'Sepia Tones' about the goddess Annapurna:

> Yes, women writers are now exploring the myths and stereotypes, a phenomenon, which has been partly influenced by the growing strength of feminist thinking. This has made it possible for us to ask a great many questions, questions which had never been asked before. Writers in India in search of some truths about themselves and their condition invariably go to the ethics and the Puranas. So do women. And when they began they were in effect rediscovering themselves, finding things relevant to their lives today.[20]

Maybe Deshpande would have liked to see Sumi develop into a writer, exploring and rediscovering herself through 'meaningful and creative reinterpretation' of myth. However, Sumi's strength is fatally crushed when she and her father Shripati are killed in a ghastly accident. The past and the present coalesce at the point of death, when Shripati takes the name of his lost son, Madhav, Sumi's brother, whose absence is the clue to the mystery of the Shripati–Kalyani relationship. The question of the necessity of Sumi's death has often been asked. Why does Sumi die? Menon suggests that if one places Gopal at the centre of the novel, then Sumi's death is inevitable, 'the cataclysmic end of happiness that Gopal had anticipated all along, death wish fulfilled'. Menon also points out that Sumi dies just when she is about to embark on her new career – her teaching job and writing – when she finds her own voice. 'Is this the moral of the story, then, that the wages of speech is death?', asks Menon.[21] The answer is as inexplicable as the epigraph to 'The River' section: 'ask not about death'. The answer may be given by Deshpande who had said that this was not a novel of family life. She was satisfied with the novel because she had been able to portray something about the women of today, she was keenly aware of the world outside and she could pick up a sense of the youth of today. The novel belongs to Aru, Deshpande having designated her its heroine and the nerve centre of the house now – 'I'm your daughter ... I'm your son' (*MT* 233). She assures the bereaved Gopal, 'we'll be alright ... don't worry about us' (*MT* 246).

The fact that *A Matter of Time* was the first novel of Deshpande's to be published in the United States became the axis of analysis for contemporary reviews. While a reviewer writing for the *Publishers Weekly* points out that 'analogies from Hindu belief and myth make clear that Deshpande writes for readers inside India first and foremost',[22] Shama Futehally, reviewing the book in India considers this aspect to be Deshpande's talent: those who call Deshapande 'a middle class' writer are paying her a great compliment; 'they are saying that her writing is inseparable from the milieu she describes ... she writes as an insider, not as a viewer'. Describing the passage in which Kalyani is thrown into a frenzy of making beds at the unexpected appearance of Sumi and her daughters, Futehally, a writer herself, says, 'such confusion, then, reflects the cultural miscellany with which we all have to cope'. Deshpande's refusal to 'explain' the complicated relationship is lauded. She 'does not try to straighten out this medley ... she merely presents it, and as closely as possible ... these stories are convincing because inarticulateness and silence of various kinds, is a deeply Indian response. We are after all a society where a range of emotions is denoted by the simple expedient "of not talking".'[23]

Almost all the reviewers compliment Deshpande's technical mastery in interweaving first- and third-person narrative and comment on the significance of the house, the pattern of the return to the natal home and other recurring themes. This strength of the women to combat the vicissitudes of their lives is observed by the reviewers – '*A Matter of Time* shatters the stereotype of Indian women as helpless, and of marriage as the only option left to them.'[24] '*A Matter of Time* ... strives to define a new and evolved center of power ... [and] the book becomes a hope, a faith, a prayer.'[25] A review in the *New York Times* observes that 'Deshpande's unadorned style refuses to call attention to itself' and that the book is written in 'an unfussy, unmagical prose', surely a compliment at a time when the use of an exoticized English language by writers in India is a much debated topic.[26]

Reviewing her works, Deshpande sees the shift in tone in *A Matter of Time* from her previous writing: 'the way I see my own work is that with *That Long Silence* I came to the end of one stage, *The Binding Vine* was a kind of trying to move on to another part. And with *A Matter of Time* I moved with greater certainty into a new area: I was trying to get a wider perspective, more outwardness and less introspection.'[27] *A Matter of Time* is a novel of love and loss and human bonding, a theme she examines in her next novel, *Small Remedies*.

6

Small Remedies

I believe that women are neither inferior nor subordinate human beings but one half of the human race. I believe that women (and men as well) should not be strait-jacketed into roles that warp their personalities, but should have options available to them. I believe that Nature, when conferring its gifts on humans, did not differentiate between males and females, except for the single purpose of procreation. I believe that motherhood does not bar everything else, but is a bonus, an extra that women are privileged to have.[1]

Small Remedies, published by Viking, Penguin India, 2000, is Deshpande's 'most confident novel', entwining the major themes of her previous novels to near perfection.[2] Deshpande says, 'in *Small Remedies*, the central idea was the writing of a biography of a person, an artist. As I wrote, I found myself exploring the idea of the many different versions of a life, and which is the true version? Or is there anything like the Truth at all?'[3] Deshpande moves away, for the first time, from the interiority of middle-class, professional, urban women, wives and mothers in the process of searching for and defining a self. Central to a novel that has more 'outwardness' and 'less stridency, less anger and less confusion' she says than her previous novels, is the story of four women, Bai, Leela, Munni and Madhu, the narrator.[4] Bai and Leela step out of strait-jacketed roles, exercise their options as individuals, pursue their dreams and achieve their potential by utilizing the gifts conferred on them by nature: 'women who reached beyond their grasp'.[5] The novel is about women artists and creativity. Deshpande, at a music recital, spoke about the ego, the *Aham*, of creative artists and writers and the conflicts which arose when the artist happened to be a woman – women are always conditioned to subdue and repress their *Aham*, their sense of self. How then, Deshpande asks, does a woman artist reconcile the aspects of being a woman and an artist?[6] The novel, spanning three generations of women (like *A Matter of Time*), also examines the schism in the public and private selves of the women protagonists, Bai, Munni, Leela and Madhu. Deshpande says, 'my novels are about women, they are about women artists ... They are not only about marital estrangement but also about love and loss. *Small Remedies* is as much about obsession – Madhu's, Bai's – as it is about love and loss. It is about words and language as well and also about truth'.[7]

The import of a story about a person no longer living is discussed in the opening pages of the novel – it brings the person back, fills the empty space with memories, conjures up the person and most significantly recreates him/her through words. Deshpande's previous works had discussed writing as a forum for women's self-expression (Jaya in *That Long Silence*, Mira in *The Binding Vine* and Sumi in *A Matter of Time*) and the necessity of recovering women's texts. The central trope of *Small Remedies* is the writing of a story, a book about a living person, an artist. Madhu, grieving for the death of her teenage son, Aditya, understands that she must go on living to find an explanation for what happened, 'to make sense of this freakish thing that happened to us, turning our lives ... into this arid desert' (*SR* 55). Like Urmi in *The Binding Vine*, who, grieving for the death of her daughter, found her salvation in transcribing Mira's poetry, Madhu accepts the offer to write the story of living legend Savitribai Indorekar (or Bai, as she is known), doyenne of Hindustani classical music and the mother of her childhood friend Munni. What follows when Madhu goes to Bhavanipur, in search of Bai's story and her self is a discussion about the meaning of biography and literature for different persons in the novel. For Yogi and Maya, commissioning the book, business rather than sentiment, is the impetus for the book on Bai: 'Fiction is dicey, poetry is out ... so we thought, why not biographies. They are always interesting and it's quite the trend now' (*SR* 19). Their interest is not so much in the woman artist and her music as in the 'controversial' aspect of her life, which would sell and which Madhu would be able to ferret out of Bai because of her childhood connection. 'An exciting novel' is how Yogi artlessly anticipates the biography to be. For Madhu, writing the biography and going to Bhavanipur is an attempt to 'rehabilitate' her self, to forget, to get away from memories and forge a new identity: 'here, I'm safe . . . in Bai's house, I'm the woman who's going to write a book on Savitribai Indorekar. Nowhere am I . . . Aditya's mother, the identity . . . I've drowned myself in for nearly eighteen years' (*SR* 153). Unable to release her self from the memories of her son, Madhu wants to learn from Bai, a mother who has successfully eradicated from memory her daughter Munni and 'silenced' every reference to her. 'Can Bai give me the clue to this? Has she found the secret?' (*SR* 155). For the subject of this biography, Bai, the work has a specific purpose. As the narrator Madhu puts it, there are three books:

> Firstly, there's Bai's book, the book Bai wants to be written, in which she is the heroine, the spotlight shining on her and her alone. No dark corners anywhere in this book, all the shadows kept out of sight, backstage.
>
> Then there's Maya and Yogi's book. A controversial one, Trendy. Politically correct, with a feminist slant. A book that will sell.
>
> And there's my book, the one I'm still looking for. It's evading me, not giving me a hold anywhere. (*SR* 125)

The problem that faces the author writing about the living artist, then, is which self to write about – as Jaya had said in *That Long Silence*, the mirror shows you ten different faces; Deshpande says there are many different versions of a life. Which one is true? The question that is analysed also relates to the personality of the narrator: would Madhu the child who knew Bai and Bai's daughter Munni, now silenced, be present in the book? Moreover, 'how do you capture a person in words?' (*SR* 162) Deshpande had said that women 'let us remember, have not participated in the process of word making'.[8] Yet as Tony, an expert in words, says, 'without words there can be no ideas, no emotions . . . wordless we are blank' (*SR* 163). Madhu, who had performed the Saraswati puja using a dictionary as a symbol of Saraswati, the goddess of learning, has to use words to contain a personality within the pages of a book; ironically, she has to use words to construct and then portray a singer to whom words are insignificant –the emotion conveyed through the swara and the raga are more important than words. 'And I have to work on her life, to sculpt with words', says Madhu about the famed singer (*SR* 164).

Madhu sets out to first 'record' Bai's life story and allows her to speak from her perspective. C. S. Lakshmi, in a fascinating work, *The Singer and the Song: Conversations with Women Musicians*, interviews women singers using 'oral history' as a methodology for the study. 'The women had to speak.' Her purpose was to 'try and understand them as women sharing a historical context, living and functioning as women and as artists, in a patriarchal society that fixed them in particular ways'.[9] The interviews of legends in classical music, vocal and instrumental, depict the conflict between traditional families and artistic aspirations. Bai's story as a singer is almost predictable. Born into a wealthy Brahmin family, she shares with her mother a love of music. Tutored by her in the sort of songs women sang then, 'aarti songs, ritual songs, stotras' (*SR* 27), the child sings before a family gathering, only to be silenced. As a daughter-in-law she is allowed to hear but not see the singers who perform in her married home. Crossing the first barrier, literally the threshold of her father-in-law's room, she pleads for music lessons and is allowed both lessons and an opportunity to attend concerts. The story of her pursuit of her Guru, Pundit Kashinath Buwa, in her determination to have him accept her as his disciple is not unusual (see note 10); after hearing him during a Ganapati festival, she pleads with him almost every day to teach her. She is told that music is no profession for a respectable married woman ('it became a curse, my being a Brahmin woman. My belonging to a respectable family').[10] She has to live in town in one room, travel each day by train and then walk two miles to Guruji's house and spend ten to twelve hours practising.

Bai's story speaks of commitment and dedication to her art, of the courage to step across the threshold and break out of the restrictions of upper caste patriarchal society in search of a dream. Her success is evident in the photographs she shows Madhu – a guided tour of her career, her performances, awards; pictures with prime ministers, singers, dancers and writers. 'She's reached the top', reflects Madhu on seeing all the pictures and listening to Bai's story. Yet this is not the whole truth. Bai's story is not just a record of dates of achievements and success: Madhu analyses this record by comparing it with her biography of Hamidbhai, in which both Hamidbhai and the narrator Madhu were absent: 'His personal life remained invisible ... I was not in the book either' (*SR* 160). Madhu decides that she will not write the hagiography that Bai expects her to write. The woman artist, self-obsessed, dominating and living for her art, has a single goal – 'it is through her music that she is reaching out to immortality, it is by putting her life on record that she hopes to live on, it is through the book that she hopes to satisfy her longing for eternal life ... to make up ... for the blanking out that is a woman's destiny after her death' (*SR* 168). The import of the recovery of women's writing and history as a testimony to their art has been dealt with in *The Binding Vine* (see also chapter 1). Yet, there are many selves and Bai as an artist is one of her myriad selves. In Madhu, for the first time Deshpande, depicts a woman narrator who is an artist fashioning and moulding the life of another artist.

> I can take over Bai's life and make what I want of it through words. I can trap her into an image I create, seal her into an identity I make for her. The power of the writer is the power of the creator. Yes, I can do much. I can make Bai the rebel who rejected the conventions of her times. The feminist who lived her life on her terms. The great artist who struggled and sacrificed everything in the cause of her art. The woman who gave up everything – a comfortable home, a husband and a family – for love. (*SR* 166)

Deshpande says writers 'belong to the race of those seeking knowledge':[11] Madhu is in search of a story that Bai refuses to give her: 'she refuses to relinquish control, to let [Madhu] have anything more than what she has decided [she] can have' (*SR* 166). However, Madhu is able to see Bai not only as Bai sees her self, a woman in search of her destiny training under Guruji, 'steady in the pursuit of her goal, pure of purpose' (*SR*

170). Madhu sees her, 'warts and all',[12] as a 'nasty, tyrannical creature' (SR 61) with her student Hasina; through Hari's eyes as living a life 'that doesn't look beyond one's own self' (SR 95); and primarily as a woman who resolutely and stubbornly holds on to her own idea of her life. Bai sees herself 'as someone unique', says Madhu sarcastically: 'she refuses to be set even in the context of other singers. The spotlight has to be on her and her alone: she is still . . . inhabiting the I-Me-Myself worlds of a child' (SR 167). Madhu refuses to swallow this bland story of public success and sets out to recover the areas of silence in Bai's life – the presence of Ghulam Saab, her Muslim lover, and Meenakshi/Munni, her daughter by Ghulam Saab, both rejected and discarded by Bai in her trajectory of success as a singer: 'there is no Munni in her life, no illegitimate child, no abandoned husband, no lover' (SR 78).

Madhu's memories of Bai relate to her avatar as her childhood friend Munni's mother. Deshpande had said motherhood 'is a bonus . . . that women are privileged to have'. Yet, Bai's silence about Munni is a dimension of her personality that Madhu the narrator and Munni's childhood friend, and Madhu the bereaved mother, has to analyse. As all these selves, Madhu now counterpoints the past and the present to negotiate her way 'between [the professional singer] and the cruel mother of [her] memory. Between this woman and the dazzlingly beautiful singer with her lover, whom she kept purposefully in the background' (SR 170).

Munni is allowed to tell her story, fiction rather, as Bai had been allowed to tell hers. A double perspective emerges, as both the adult and now more discerning narrator, Madhu, and the reader are able to see two contrasting selves emerge. The daughter of Bai and Ghulam Saab, the child maintains the fiction that her father, a Hindu lawyer, lives in Pune, conjures a picture of a palatial home and concocts the story of her kidnapping. She draws an image of Ghulam Saab as a cruel man and dismisses his presence in her mother's life as easily as Bai was to later dismiss both her daughters and her lovers. She decries music – 'I hate music . . . I simply hate it' (SR 135). The one person she cannot deny in her childhood is her mother Savitribai. Bai, however, ruthlessly pursues her ambitions, privileging her career as a singer over her role as mother.

Madhu remembers her 'walking on without a backward look at the child hovering in the shadows, the child who was waiting . . . for a word from her mother, a glance. Any kind of recognition of her presence. A recognition which is still being denied' (SR 169). The motherless child, Madhu, and Munni, the child neglected by her mother, bond in a strange way, their friendship ending when Munni, all knowing about love and sex, informs Madhu about her father's mistress (Munni and Madhu join a league of Deshpande's women protagonists who are in distant or troubled relationship with their mother and closer to their father – Saru, Jaya and Urmi). Munni's story is completed by Madhu, who feels responsible as narrator to fill the gaps in Bai's story, to recover the text of Munni's life and to end the silence enveloping the subject of Munni.

In a movement that is in contrast to the daughters who reflect their mothers – Saru in *The Dark Holds No Terrors*, Mira in *The Binding Vine* and Sumi in *A Matter of Time* – Munni patterns herself as an antithesis to her mother. If Bai strove for a life of success as a dazzlingly beautiful singer, Munni strove for a life of ordinariness and anonymity: 'she yearned for the conventional life Bai had found so stultifying' (SR 169). By naming her Meenakshi Indorekar, Bai had delinked her daughter from her father Ghulam Saab and her husband. Munni renames and recasts her self, 'beating herself into shape with a savage determination, like dough being pounded into soft pliability' (SR 225). As Bai had stepped across the threshold and had made a decision to chalk out her life as the singer, so Munni takes a decision to chart her life. She calls herself Shailaja Joshi, 'looks like any other middle class Bombay housewife, more overweight than most' (SR 76), with short greying hair and the signs of an ordinary domestic life – a bunch of keys at her waist and a plastic bag at her feet, travelling in a bus (in contrast to the pearl and chiffon clad Bai in a car). The 'Mangalsutra' around her neck, a symbol of married life that a Hindu woman might wear, completes the metamorphosis of the daughter of the famed Bai and her Muslim lover. Munni wanted respectability and so rejected everything associated with her mother – 'music, genius, ambition, freedom' – 'closed herself against her mother' (SR 224–5). Ironically, the notice of Munni's death proclaims her the daughter of Savitribai, though her wedding card had announced the names only of her father and grandfather, 'the mother's name nowhere' (SR 283). The notice of her death, Madhu feels, gave her back the identity she had denied all her life.

The puzzle of Munni's absence from Bai's story is solved when Madhu realizes that Munni had severed the umbilical cord with her mother. Aditya's mother, Madhu who had branded Bai the 'lowest, meanest kind of creature' (SR 78) for denying her child, now realizes that it was Munni who had denied her mother. As the novel proceeds, Madhu sees the many selves of Bai as she discovers an understanding of women who courageously exercise options and refuse to be strait-jacketed.

Linked to Bai's story is the story of Ghulam Saab, the Muslim tabla player, the only male artist to be allowed into Savitribai's music lessons and the man with whom she elopes in search of her destiny. In the Ghulam–Savitri relationship, Deshpande, perhaps for the first time, suggests a story of love outside marriage. The relationships of Saru and Boozie, Jaya and Kamat, and Urmi and Bhaskar never developed, as Deshpande's focus was on the inner journey of her women protagonists. Bai, however, elopes, 'a step so great that even today it would require enormous courage. The stuff even movies still hesitate to take on' (SR 166). Ghulam Saab's devotion and love for Bai is captured in photographs where Madhu notices that every artist is looking into the camera except for Ghulam Saab, whose eyes are fixed on Bai. Significantly, because Bai does not mention him, Ghulam Saab's story is pieced together by Madhu's remembrance of the courteous, kind and elegant man of her childhood, and Hasina's story of the artist, the incomparable tabla player. While Bai pursued her art with Guruji, Ghulam supported her in every way – met people, arranged programmes and made contacts. Bai's success as a singer was dependent on the support provided by Ghulam Saab; yet there is complete silence about him in Bai's story. Munni's quest for respectability, reflected in her donning of the Mangalsutra as a sign of being a married Hindu woman, is duplicated in Bai's quest for respectability as well. She appears on stage as Savitribai Indorekar, doyenne of the

Gwalior Gharana of music, wearing a Mangalsutra. Having achieved her dream of success as a classical singer, Bai, perhaps seeks to reclaim respectability: 'a respectably married woman. Both Ghulam Saab, her lover, and Munni, her daughter, no longer part of her life' (*SR* 167).

Madhu, who had set out determined to write Bai's biography, which included Munni and Ghulam's story, realizes that all facets of a personality – Jaya's ten different faces in the mirror – may coexist. She sees varied and differing pictures of Munni, Bai and Ghulam Saab; 'which is the true version?', asks Deshpande, 'or is there anything like the truth at all?' Madhu can see

> a complex, complicated human being who comes to [her] through words . . . an artist, a musician . . . there are times when she falters and then . . . [she gets] a certain glimpse of a human being behind that shield . . . it's in this darkness that the woman [she wants] resides. Her silences about her personal life, about her life with her husband, with her lover, her muteness about the hardships she suffered as a woman who flouted the rules of society – these are what link her to that woman. (*SR* 177)

Madhu comes to an understanding of a woman who could step out of a stereotypical role to achieve her dream even at the cost of giving up something. There is a grudging admiration for a woman who does not complain about the problems in her professional life because they were part of the road she had chosen, the choice she had exercised. In Madhu's depiction of Bai, Deshpande presents a woman who was 'as unaware of trendy feminism as she [was] of political correctness' (*SR* 167). Deshpande's portrayal of Bai is linked to her memory of her childhood in Dharwar, when she would hear the sound of music filtering through a house she used to walk by. Existing outside the pages of feminist anthologies, Bai's story is the story of many a classical singer in India who has crossed the threshold.

Madhu's understanding of Bai is significantly linked with her own coming to terms with Aditya's death. Obsessed with her love for her son, Madhu had subsumed every aspect of her personality to playing the role of a mother. The long passages on her monomania with motherhood almost duplicate what

Deshpande says about motherhood as a male construct and a construct of myth and legend, distinct from reality. Madhu's silence about being assaulted when she was 15 years old by her father's artist friend, and the inexplicable wrath of her husband, Som, unleashes a chain of events, which culminates in Aditya's death in a bomb blast, linked to the violence between Hindus and Muslims in the aftermath of the demolition of the Babri Masjid. Madhu's story from her childhood till this crisis is also a story of survival and resilience. Deshpande portrays Madhu's inner journey in the context of the stories of Bai, Munni and Leela. Her understanding of the many selves that may coexist like a palimpsest, none erased, is linked to the story of Leela.

Leela, her mother's sister, is seen by Madhu as her guardian, and protector, as a mother figure who had looked after her and brought her out of the terrifying emptiness of her father's death and who was there for her after her son's death. The Leela that Madhu knows is a widow who could not speak English and who married the Christian doctor Joe (the Brahmin widow married to the Christian Joe reflects the Brahmin singer Bai and her Muslim lover Ghulam Saab). The 'other' self of Leela, the public self, is not known to Madhu. During the course of the novel, Madhu discovers the story of Leela through Hari. The widowed Leela had refused to return to her father's house and to a life of comfortable domesticity and anonymity. She had instead crossed the threshold and joined the Communist Party. She had both economic independence and a room of her own in Maruti Chawl, from where she supported the striking mill and railway workers, and women afflicted with TB. Significantly, Leela's achievements are blanked out and never spoken about till Hari 'recovers' the text of her public life. Madhu can see two Leelas – Hari's 'Leela is the public figure: my Leela is the woman who made me part of her life' (*SR* 98). Madhu's narrative is able to reconcile the many selves and link Bai to Leela. 'I've been thinking that in writing about Bai, I am writing about Leela as well . . . women who reached beyond their grasp. Bai moving out of her class in search of her destiny as a singer, Leela breaking out of the conventions of widowhood, reaching out from her small room to the world looking for justice for the weak' (*SR* 284).

84

Small Remedies is the first of Deshpande's novels to present women, Bai and Leela who break through the stereotypical mould and chart a different course in their lives. The technique of the narrator who, coping with a crisis and in search of metaphysical meaning, finds it in the personality and works of an artist, had already been dealt with in Urmi's recovery of Mira's poem in *The Binding Vine*. The silences and the stories of women that remain 'blanketed' is a theme that Deshpande had also been dealing with in her previous novels. Her women protagonists in quest of a definition of their selves had found meaning within the structure of a family. While using the recurring technique of first-person narrative and the counter-pointing of past and present, *Small Remedies* charts new territories in its depictions of Bai and Leela. While the previous novels had dealt with the trope of ending a silence and speaking or writing, *Small Remedies* is a novel about music and community work. The women, Bai, Leela, Munni, Madhu and later Hasina, are still centre-stage; other than Ghulam Saab and the warm-hearted Tony, the men, Som, Chandru and Hari, remain shadowy – as Deshpande says, 'in the wings'.

The ending of *Small Remedies* is almost spectacular in contrast to the more conventional endings of the previous novels. Set in Bhavanipur temple, in memory of Guruji, it brings together Guruji, Savitri, Ghulam Saab, and Hasina as a student of all three, in a single tradition. More significantly, Hasina, a Muslim woman, first sings the Devi stotra, a Shankaracharya shloka in praise of Annapurna that the Hindu priest had performed the puja with. Later she sings a bhajan, an Akka Mahadevi vachana that Bai had never been able to bring her self to sing, unable to give to a bhajan the devotion and selflessness it required. 'Now her student Hasina, a Muslim woman, sings this poem, composed centuries ago by a woman, a Hindu woman, whose entire life was a statement of her faith'. The ending is appropriate, coming as it does after opposition to a Muslim singing and an account of the Hindu–Muslim riots and the bomb explosion that killed both Aditya, Madhu's son, and Munni, Bai's daughter. Deshpande portrays for the first time an issue of significant national concern, the schism between the Hindu and Muslim communities. She had tried earlier, she says, to deal with national issues, particularly in *That Long Silence* – but, while they did contain references to strikes and agitations, Deshpande's novels had remained within the ambit of the home.

Deshpande often compares her technique of writing to music: when asked about her motivation for writing she talks about self-expression: 'There is something I want to say, something is there in me which wants to come out like music. Nobody creates music for the sake of doing something. It is there in you, and it comes out. . . . in the writing . . . there is a craftsmanship . . . just like in music'. *Small Remedies* is the perfect example of this blend.

7

Conclusion

The issue of Indian writing in English is a much debated topic. English was institutionalized as a language in Macaulay's Minutes on Education in 1835 and imposed as a medium of higher education in colonial India. The Indian living languages were dismissed as 'dialects' which contain 'neither literary nor scientific information, and are moreover, so poor and rude, that until they are enriched from another quarter, it will not be easy to translate any valuable work into them'.[1] Scholars have, since, drawn a link between the institutionalization of the English language and literature, on the one hand, and the imperialists' quest for greater power and control, on the other, 'between the process of curricular selection and the impulse to dominate and control'.[2] Today, English is a language spoken by millions of Indians, the medium of instruction for education and one of the official languages ratified by the Indian Constitution. Which language is Indian, or which language should Indian writers write in – the vernacular or English – is a complex question, as even today English seems to be linked with the notion of power and privilege. The international success of Salman Rushdie's *Midnight's Children*, the subsequent international visibility of Indian writing in English, and Rushdie's selection of only writing in English for a volume commemorating India's fiftieth year of independence, brought out in the open a polarity between regional writing and writing in English. The question of the 'authenticity' of a literature written in a 'foreign' language imposed by the colonialists with a subversive intent has elicited varied responses from Indian writers. Hindi writer Rajendra Yadav says, 'If I have to write for English readers then I have to go into tedious explanations ... That's why Indian writing in English is so second-rate . It's circumscribed by what the western reader can appreciate: exotica or erotica. The IWE take a touristy look at India. ... It's a creatively-written traveler's guide ... their total approach is to Westerners: a third-rate serpent-and-rope trick.'

Indian writing in English has been seen as a literature specifically written for a western readership. 'There is always a temptation when you think or write in English not to penetrate the psyche of the Indian people but instead write for the West ... It makes both the IWE and their readers intellectual pygmies,' says Punjabi writer Gurdial Singh. IWE, written in a language that does not specifically belong to a region, has been characterized as a literature written in a cultural vacuum or written by diasporic writers. Tamil writer Ashokamitran says, 'I have a greater advantage because I have a country, a language, a community,' even as Hindi writer Nirmal Verma asserts that his language links him to 'a tradition of 5,000 years, to the medieval writers, to the Bhakti poets, to the Sanskrit classics and also connects [him] to the philosophical texts of Indian culture. But English writers are deprived of all this unless they are very sensitive.'[3] The debate between the regional writers and writers in English centring on the language, its authenticity in a muti-lingual society and its regional/cultural base has widened in recent times.

Deshpande's response to the accusations in 'an open letter to some fellow writers' only reiterates a stand she has taken for years. Writing in English does not alienate her from her roots, she says, or invalidate her experience: 'This is our home, as it is yours; we did not drop out of the skies when we started writing in English ... My father was a Kannada writer, my mother came from Pune, my husband comes from a rural landed family: my self encompasses all these, it is out of this self that I write.'[4] Deshpande saw the birth of an independent nation and, in 'Them and Us', published in *Unbecoming Daughters of the Empire*, recalls a childhood spent reciting both English rhymes and Sanskrit *shlokas*; 'the idea of an Empire somehow seeped into us ... we did sums that went "John has 10 apples and Tom has five," learnt poems about strange things like tuffets and muffins, daffodils and daisies ... sang

"Simple Simon met a pieman" (pieman?) ... and on all ceremonial occasions we sang "God save the King" ... (but at home we) entered a different world altogether. There were neither apples nor daisies here; instead we ate mangoes and guavas and plucked jasmine buds.'[5]

Deshpande's father, a renowned Sanskrit scholar and a famous Kannada playwright taught her Sanskrit every evening and was 'forever, in moments of leisure, absentmindedly and tunelessly intoning verses from the Gita, from Kalidas and the songs of the saint – poets in Kannada'.[6] There seemed to be no contradiction in Deshpande's childhood years between study-ing in an English school, listening to and reciting Sanskrit *shlokas* and speaking in Kannada and Marathi. Childhood play fused cultural archetypes – 'the combination never seemed odd. We did it too. Shakuntala and Dushyanta and a princess who ate rice and curds were as familiar to us as Heidi and Alice ... When we performed a play at home ... we did a scene from *Pygmalion* (... and I was, I remember, Eliza Doolittle, adding, no doubt, another brand of spoken English to Shaw's list!) and another about an Indian princess and a beggar girl which we took from one of our school texts.'[7] The option of sending Deshpande to study in an English school when most parents sent their children to the regional language school was taken by her father despite his great love for his own language and literature, maybe also because of his 'admiration for Western, specially English ideas, language and literature'.[8] The number and range of books lining the book-shelves at home inculcated her reading habits in childhood. Reading, she says, was as necessary as breathing or eating and the atmosphere at home created a 'world of words and ideas [she] was happily submerged in'. By the time she was seven or eight, 'English became [her] language'. 'I read enormously, from children books to Jane Austen, the Brontës, Dickens, George Eliot, Hardy: before I was out of school I had gone through them all ... I read romances and detective novels in my teens, Enid Blyton only with my children ... Home was a harmonious mixture of languages ... Nevertheless, all reading was in English.'[9] It was only later, when Deshpande came to a consciousness of herself as a feminist after writing *That Long Silence*, that she read western feminists – 'Simone de Beauvoir,

Germaine Greer, Betty Friedan, Kate Millet, Virginia Woolf – whose *A Room of One's Own*, along with Simone de Beauvoir's The *Second Sex*, have been the greatest influence on me.' However, she is quick to point out that these books were only confirmatory; 'my idea of feminism came to me out of my own life, my own experiences and thinking'.[10]

The choice to write in English was natural: 'English was and remained the language of my thinking, it was the language in which I expressed myself. Therefore when I began to write I wrote in English. There was no question of choice. . . . the answer is a very simple one. I write in English because it is the only language I can express myself in.'[11] In a recent unpublished article Deshpande reiterates her position on this unequivocally: 'I began writing in English, not because I "chose" to but because it was the only language I could write and express myself in, the only language I really read. Yet I had two other languages at home, languages I spoke and lived my daily life in.'[12] Deshpande in earlier articles has acknowledged the difficulties of writing in English particularly when she has to use untranslatable words. She has written extensively on the complexity of using English as a medium of expression by non-English speaking characters in her novels. 'Dialogues are also difficult. Different people use language in different ways, depending on caste, class, region, generation and gender. You can't convey all this in English.'[13] The issue is complicated by the fact that, while she thinks in English, her emotional expressions are formed in her own language. She admits to reworking an enormous amount. making up to seven drafts of each novel to perfect the language.

It was another aspect of writing in English that troubled her – the sense of isolation, of not 'belonging' to a writers group, or a literary tradition. Not only did Deshpande feel alienated from the non-English Indian culture and literature, but she did not feel a sense of literary kinship with the IWE writers of the time either. 'The only common factor was that we were Indians and that we wrote in English. And so in a sense I wrote in a vacuum.'[14] In recent years, as IWE came into its own and gained international recognition, the divide between the languages has provoked Deshpande's response in articles and conference papers. She refuses to be one of those writers who 'generally don't trouble themselves with academic questions about their writings; they just write and leave the rest to academics and critics'.[15] In a recent unpublished article, 'Where do we Belong: Regional, National, or International', she has linked the notion of language with the question of identity and readership. While categorically stating that English writing in India is very much part of the vast and complex literary scene of the country, one of the literatures that forms the mosaic of what is called Indian literature, Deshpande asserts that her writing is as 'authentic' as her father's.

> And being what I was, the daughter of a Kannada writer, and feeling, therefore, part of that literary world as well, how could I think of myself, or my writing which came out of that society, the same milieu, as alien? No, I have never had any doubts that my writing was as much a part of the Indian Literature as my father's was. And therefore my conviction that writing in English is as much a part of the literatures of this country as the writing in any other language.[16]

In the article, Deshpande moves beyond the pale of confrontation and defence of the language, and seeks to analyse the development of IWE in recent times. She sees a recent surge of self-confidence among the writers, both in their use of language and in their sense of identity. Now writers write in English, not as 'Indian' writers carrying the burden of conveying a pan-India consciousness, but as Tamilians, Bengalis, Punjabis, Keralites, 'to write as naturally as if they were writing in their own languages'. Moreover, novels are no longer situated in 'nowhere land', Deshpande says, quoting Ritu Menon on the 'National-Geographic-land-and-its-people kind of treatment', but in Mumbai, Calcutta, Bangalore, Coorg and so on 'i.e. a definite place in a definite region. In effect, we are witnessing the emergence of the regional novel in English.'

Deshpande has no fears about the future of writing in English. 'I am convinced from my own experience that English does not distance us from our own creative source, that a language cannot by itself create a gap between a text and the culture it belongs to.' The writer who has rejected labels – 'Asian writer, Indo-English, Indian writer in English, third world writer, postcolonial writer and so on' – stresses that her writings must be understood in the right context:

It is critics who need to widen their understanding, to learn to contextualise correctly, to shake off the vestiges of Colonialism that makes them ignore the source and context of our writing and link it to another literature only because the two share a common language. In other words we need to stop looking at ourselves through the eyes of those 'others', and see ourselves with our own eyes, instead. The main problem seems to be the lack of powerful voices in this country, voices that will speak with authority, knowledge and sensitivity to our concerns. What we have instead is a toeing of the line drawn by critics and academics abroad, who seem to have no idea of the context to which we belong, what we have is a parroting of the latest theory that comes from outside. . . . Unfortunately, English writing in our country must be the only literature in the world in which the opinions of the critics outweigh the criticism and even the responses of the readers within the country . . . To affirm our own reality, to write about it without reference to whether or not it is acceptable to the West, is part of the project of the recovery of that lost self-esteem. [17]

Notes

CHAPTER 1. INTRODUCTION

1. Shashi Deshpande, 'Of Concerns, Of Anxieties', Indian Literature: Women's Writing in English, *New Voices*, 175, 39:5 (September–October 1996), 107, 110, 109.
2. Meenakshi Mukherjee, *The Perishable Empire: Essays in Indian Writings in English* (New Delhi: Oxford University Press, 2000), 15–16.
3. Aijaz Ahmad, *In Theory: Classes, Nations, Literatures* (London: Verso 1987).
4. Amrita Basu, (ed.), *The Challenge of Local Feminisms: Women's Movements in Global Perspective* (New Delhi: Kali for Women, 1999), 19.
5. Basu, *Challenge of Local Feminisms*, 3.
6. All discussions on patriarchy are from Kamla Bhasin's, *What is Patriarchy?* (New Delhi: Kali for Women, 1993). See also, in Kali Primaries, Kamla Bhasin's *Understanding Gender* and *Some Questions on Feminism and its Relevance in South Asia*.
7. Uma Chakravarti, 'Conceptualizing Brahmanical Patriarchy in Early India: Gender, Caste, Class and State', *Economic and Political Weekly*, 1993. Quoted in Bhasin, *What is Patriarchy?*, 36.
8. Ibid., 37.
9. Kumkum Sangari and Sudesh Vaid (eds.), *Recasting Women: Essays in Colonial History* (New Delhi: Kali for Women, 1989), 3. The discussion in this section relies on articles from this excellent collection on the role of women in colonial India.
10. Quoted by Uma Chakravarti in 'Whatever Happened to the Vedic Dasi?: Orientalism, Nationalism and a Script for the Past', in Sangari and Vaid, *Recasting Women*, 35.
11. Mrinalini Sinha, *Colonial Masculinity: The 'manly Englishman' and the 'effeminate Bengali' in the late Nineteenth Century* (New Delhi: Kali for Women, 1997).

12. Lata Mani, 'Contentious Traditions: The Debate on Sati in Colonial India', in Sangari and Vaid, *Recasting Women*, 88–126.
13. Sinha, *Colonial Masculinity*, 45.
14. Quoted by Uma Chakravarti in Sangari and Vaid, *Recasting Women*, 51.
15. Sinha, *Colonial Masculinity*, 46.
16. Tanika Sarkar, *Words to Win: The Making of 'Amar Jiban': A Modern Autobiography* (New Delhi: Kali for Women, 1999), 30. See also pp. 25–31.
17. Ibid., 75–6.
18. Ibid., 78–9.
19. Swami Vivekananda, quoted by Chakravarti in *Recasting Women*, 77.
20. M. K. Gandhi, from *Harijan*, 24 February 1940 and *Young India*, 11 August 1921.
21. Radha Kumar, *The History of Doing: An Illustrated Account of Movements for Women's Rights and Feminism in India, 1800–1990* (New Delhi: Kali for Women, 1993), 2. All discussions in this section are from this book.
22. Quoted in Kumar, *History of Doing*, 50.
23. Ibid., 1.
24. Ibid., 3.
25. Vrinda Nabar, *Caste as Woman* (New Delhi: Penguin Books, 1995).
26. Malashri Lal, *The Law of the Threshold: Women Writers in Indian English* (Shimla: Indian Institute of Advanced Study, 1995).
27. Vikram Chandra in *Stree: A Tribute to the Indian Woman*, a special edition of *Outlook* (n.d.), 139.
28. Elaine Showalter, *A Literature of their Own: British Women Novelists from Brontë to Lessing* (1977; London: Virago Press, 1982), 9.
29. From Maggie Humm (ed.), *Feminisms: A Reader* (London: Harverster Wheatsheaf, 1992), and Mary Eagleton (ed.), *Feminist Literary Theory: A Reader* (Oxford: Blackwell Publishers, 1986).
30. Ibid.
31. Bill Ashcroft, Garreth Griffiths and Helen Tiffin (eds.), *The Post-Colonial Studies Reader* (London and New York: Routledge, 1995), 3.
32. From 'Under Western Eyes: Feminist Scholarship and Colonial Discourses, Third World Women and the Politics of Feminism', in Eagleton, *Feminist Literary Theory*, 390, 392.
33. Susie Tharu and K. Lalita (eds.), *Women Writing in India: 600 B.C. to the Present*, vol. 2, *The Twentieth Century* (New Delhi: Oxford University Press, 1993), 25.
34. Ibid.

35. Ibid., 34.
36. Ibid., 38 and 39.
37. Ibid., 40.
38. Lakshmi Holmström (ed.), *The Inner Courtyard: Stories by Indian Women* (London: Virago Press, 1990; New Delhi: Rupa, 1991), xi–xii.
39. Lal, *Law of the Threshold*, 12.
40. Ibid., 13.
41. Ibid., 28; emphasis in original.
42. Shashi Deshpande, 'The Indian Woman – Myths, Stereotypes and Reality' (private papers, 1977). An adaptation published as the Afterword to *The Stone Women* (Calcutta: Writers Workshop, 2000), 85–95.
43. Ibid.
44. Shashi Deshpande, 'Where Do We Belong? The "Problem" of English in India', *Kunapipi: Journal of Post Colonial Writing*, 19:3 (1997), 72.

CHAPTER 2. THE DARK HOLDS NO TERRORS

1. Shashi Deshpande, 'The Indian Woman – Myths, Stereotypes and the Reality'.
2. In Romita Choudhury, 'Interview with Shashi Deshpande', *World Literature Written in English*, 34:2 (1995), 16.
3. Shashi Deshpande, 'The Power Within', in *Creating Theory: Writers on Writing*, ed. Jasbir Jain (Delhi: Pencraft, n.d.), 210. From a talk given at the Sahitya Akademi New Delhi, February 1996.
4. Shashi Deshpande, 'Of Concerns, Of Anxieties', 108.
5. From a private conversation with the author in Bangalore, 2000.
6. *The Dhammapada*, trans. Narada Thera (London: John Murray, 1954).
7. Shashi Deshpande, *The Dark Holds No Terrors* (New Delhi: Penguin Books, 1990), 28. Page references are from this edition. First published by Vikas Publishers, 1980.
8. 'The Indian Woman – Myths, Stereotypes and the Reality'.
9. Draupadi in the epic the *Mahabharata* is won by Arjuna in a Swayamavar, a contest of eligible men for the hand of the princess, and married to all five Pandavas in deference to their mother Kunti's wishes. She is offered as a stake in a gambling match between the cousins – the Kauravas and the Pandavas – and disrobed in the Assembly, these events then leading to the great war, the Mahabharata. Her story has been interpreted in folktales and stories – oral and written literature. Deshpande, in

'The Indian Woman – Myths, Stereotypes and the Reality', refers to the story of Draupadi as told by Mahasweta Devi and translated into English by Gayatri Spivak as 'one of the most powerful stories written by a woman . . . [and] also I imagine the most known'. Sita, married to Rama, in the epic the *Ramayana*, accompanies him in exile for fourteen years in the forest from where she is abducted by Ravana. She is seen as a symbol of devotion, loyalty and purity. She passes the test of fire to prove her purity and unquestioningly goes into self exile on her purity being doubted by a commoner. Shakuntala, pregnant by the king, is publicly rejected by him after a curse makes him forget her. She goes back to the king after he comes looking for her.

10. Deshpande has written on the myth of motherhood and the stereotypical qualities associated with it. Myth and movies have propagated the role of the competent, noble, 'loving, ever forgiving, sacrificing mother', an image hard to ascribe to. She quotes Mahasweta Devi's story 'Wet Nurse': 'Such is the chemistry of the soil of this land that all women turn into mothers here and all men choose to be eternal sons' ('The Indian Woman – Myths, Stereotypes and the Reality'. See also note on mothers in n. 4, Ch. 4, p. 98.

11. Meenakshi Mukherjee, 'Ghosts from the Past', *The Book Review*, March–April 1981.

12. Deshpande takes up the issue of rape in her interview with Romita Choudhury and 'In Conversation' with Sue Dickman.

13. 'The Indian Woman – Myths, Stereotypes and the Reality'.

14. See Choudhury, 'Interview with Shashi Deshpande', 19.

15. Ibid, 23.

16. Ibid., 16, 20 and 22.

17. Ibid., 23.

CHAPTER 3. THAT LONG SILENCE

1. In Choudhury, 'Interview with Shashi Deshpande', 19–20.

2. Deshpande, 'The Indian Woman – Myths, Stereotypes and the Reality'.

3. Deshpande, 'Of Concerns, Of Anxieties', 108.

4. In Choudhury, 'Interview with Shashi Deshpande', 19.

5. Deshpande, 'Of Concerns, Of Anxieties', 108.

6. These issues are elaborated upon later in *The Binding Vine*, in which Mira expresses herself in her poetry, and in *Small Remedies*, in which Bai, the celebrated unconventional singer, and Leela, the

Communist Party worker refuse to conform, and express themselves in classical music and social work.

7. Shashi Deshpande, *That Long Silence* (New Delhi: Penguin India,
   1989), 7; first published by Virago Press, London, 1988. Page
   references are from this edition.

8. From the staid *Women's Era* to *Femina*, magazines to which
   Deshpande had contributed her short stories, to a plethora of
   high-fashion magazines aimed at shaping the modern, urban
   woman in a specific way, the Indian market is flooded with
   women's magazines.

9. The renaming of the woman is Deshpande's favourite device to
   convey the remoulding of a woman after marriage in the
   conventions of the husband's family. Based on a traditional ritual,
   it finds poetic expression in Mira's poems in *The Binding Vine*.
   Mira is named Nirmala and even the radical Leela is named
   Sindhu after marriage in *Small Remedies*.

10. Deshpande, 'The Indian Woman – Myths , Stereotypes and the
    Reality'.

11. The story of silence came to Deshpande with Vimla's death. In a
    private conversation, Deshpande and I had discussed the silences
    of even educated women who either neglected their health or
    kept secret the news of their illnesses. The discussion centred on
    recent television serials, which have glorified and made devi-like
    such women who represent *Shakti* and self-control.

12. Ritu Menon, Afterword to *A Matter of Time* (New York: CUNY,1999).

13. In the epic, Mahabharata, Gandhari is the wife of the blind king
    Dhritarashtra and mother to the ninety-nine Kauravas who
    fought the epic war with the Pandavas. To share her husband's
    blind condition she bandaged her eyes for the rest of her life. She
    is an example of complete devotion to her husband and efface-
    ment of her self. See R. K. Narayan's *The Indian Epics Retold: The
    Ramayana, The Mahabharata, Gods, Demons and Others* (New Delhi:
    Penguin India, 2000).

14. Deshpande, 'The Indian Woman – Myths, Stereotypes and the
    Reality'.

15. In Choudhury, 'Interview with Shashi Deshpande', 20.

16. The extent of freedom women allowed themselves in self-
    expression and the restraint they imposed on their writings was
    the topic of ten workshops conducted between 1999 and 2001
    with 175 women writers in ten Indian languages. Published as a
    report, *The Guarded Tongue: Women's Writing and Censorship in
    India* (Secundrabad: Women's World, Asmita, 2001).

17. In Choudhury, 'Interview with Shashi Deshpande', 20.

18. Ibid., 21.
19. Ibid., 23.
20. Ibid., 25.
21. Ibid., 19.
22. Ibid., 24.
23. The Bhagvad-Gita . In a talk on her father, 'Adya Sriranga: Writer and Father', in Bangalore on 24 September 2000, Deshpande quoted these lines and said that her father had never directed her and had allowed her to take her decisions.
24. From Susie Tharu and K. Lalita (eds.), *Women's Writing in India: 600 B.C. to the Present*, vol. 2, *The Twentieth Century* (New Delhi: Oxford University Press, 1993).
25. Hema Nair, interview with Shashi Deshpande for Little India.com, October 1999.
26. Adele King, 'Effective Portrait', *Debonair*, June 1988, 7.
27. Vrinda Nabar, 'Middle-Class Lives', *The Indian Post*, 5 June 1988.
28. Maria Couto, 'In Divided Times', *Times Literary Supplement*, 1 April 1988.
29. 'Dear Reader', *Indian Review of Books*, 16 February 2000, 22.
30. In Choudhury, 'Interview with Shashi Deshpande', 16.
31. Shama Futehally, 'Of That Elusive Self', *The Book Review*, August 1989, 31.
32. In Choudhury, 'Interview with Shashi Deshpande', 25–6.
33. Vrinda Nabar, 'Words ... Language ... and Truth', *Sunday Observer*, 9 April 2000.

CHAPTER 4. THE BINDING VINE

1. Shashi Deshpande, 'Dear Reader', *Indian Review of Books*, 16 February 2000, 22.
2. Shashi Deshpande (private papers).
3. Lakshmi Holmström, 'Of Love and Loss', *Indian Review of Books*, 3:1 (16 October–15 November 1993), 52–3.
4. Deshpande, 'The Indian Woman – Myths, Stereotypes and the Reality'. Deshpande discusses the myth of motherhood, and the stereotypical assumptions associated with it, as a male construct. Movies, from the iconic *Mother India* to present-day Indian films have invariably glorified the role of the mother and invested her with superhuman powers. But rarely are mothers depicted realistically, Deshpande feels, 'warts and all'. 'We had to wait for women to write and bring out the truths of their relationship.'.
5. Shashi Deshpande, *The Binding Vine* (New Delhi: Penguin Books, 1993), 47. All page references are from this edition.

6. Deshpande, 'The Indian Woman – Myths, Stereotypes and the Reality'. See also note 4.
7. Deshpande had read Virginia Woolf – 'whose *A Room of one's Own* along with Simone de Beauvoir's *The Second Sex* have been the greatest influence on me' – but affirms that these books were 'only confirmatory'. Her idea of feminism came to her from her life, her experiences and thinking. See 'Of Concerns, Of Anxieties', 108.
8. Deshpande has written extensively on the use of English in writing fiction. For many years, however, Deshpande felt that, while she thought in English, her emotional expressions were formed in her own language. 'But when it comes to emotions, particularly when they are not expressed, when they are still inside me, they are usually in my own language' See Choudhury, 'Interview with Shashi Deshpande', 17. Also see Conclusion, pp. 87–92.
9. Deshpande, 'The Indian Woman – Myths, Stereotypes and the Reality'.
10. Deshpande, 'Dear Reader'.
11. Mrinal Pande, 'Recollecting Motherhood', in Jehanara Wasi and Malashri Lal (eds.), *A Storehouse of Tales: Contemporary Indian Women Writers* (New Delhi: Srishti, 2001), 133.
12. A leading Indian psychologist Sudhir Kakar, in *The Inner World* (1978), says that women are much less sentimental about mothers and have a more realistic idea of the relationship. Quoted by Shashi Deshpande in 'The Indian Woman – Myths, Stereotypes and the Reality'.
13. In Choudhury, 'Interview with Shashi Deshpande', 22.
14. Ibid., 25.
15. Ibid.
16. Holmström, 'Of Love and Loss', 52–3.
17. Adele King, review of *The Binding Vine*, *World Literature Today*, 68:2. (Spring 1994), 430.
18. Choudhury, 'Interview with Shashi Deshpande', 17.
19. Maria Couto, 'Bombay Talkie', review of *The Binding Vine*.
20. Shashi Deshpande, 'No (Hu) man is an Island' (private papers); appeared in *The Times of India*, 23 April 1992.

CHAPTER 5. A MATTER OF TIME

1. Interview with Sue Dickman, in Malashri Lal, Alamgir Hashmi and Victor J. Ramraj (eds.), *Post Independence Voices in South Asian Writings* (New Delhi: Doaba House, 2000), 131–2.

2. Review of *A Matter of Time* by Kirti Jain, *The Book Review*, 21:6 (June 1997), 20.

3. Chandra Holm, interview with Shashi Deshpande, 30 October 1997. Website <http://www.dharwad.com/nimmaputa/shashi. html>.

4. Lakshmi Holmström, *Wasafiri*, 17 (Spring 1993), 25.

5. Shame Futehally, in her review of *A Matter of Time* (*The Hindu*, 19 June 1997), says that 'according to my arithmetic, this is Shashi Deshpande's fourth important novel, coming as it does after *The Dark Holds no Terror, That Long Silence* and *The Binding Vine* ... in terms of time, Deshpande's writing spans over twenty years ... it is a very substantial body of work'.

6. As told to Ritu Menon for the Afterword to *A Matter of Time* (New York: CUNY, 1999), 254. Hereafter referred to as Menon.

7. Menon, 252.

8. Ibid.

9. The Brhad-aranyaka Upanishad, the most important Upanishad, consisting of three sections: the *Madhu Kanda*, which expounds the teaching of the basic identity of the individual and the Universal Self; the *Yajnavalkaya* or the *Muni Kanda*, which provides a philosophical justification of the teaching, and the *Khila Kanda*, which deals with certain modes of worship and meditation. See *The Principal Upanishad*, ed. S. Radhakrishnan (London: George Allen and Unwin, 1953), 146.

10. Holmström, *Wasafiri*, 23.

11. Shashi Deshpande, *A Matter of Time* (New Delhi: Penguin India, 1996), 71; hereafter referred to as *MT*. Page numbers are included in the text.

12. Kamla Bhasin, *Understanding Gender* (New Delhi: Kali for Women, 2000), 30.

13. Shauna Singh Baldwin's *What the Body Remembers* deals with the practice in India of marrying a second time to produce a male heir – a practice which continued until the Indian government pronounced bigamy illegal in the Hindu Marriage Act.

14. Interview with Dickman, p. 132–3.

15. Ibid., 134.

16. Menon, 259.

17. Ibid., 258.

18. Ibid.

19. Futehally, review of *A Matter of Time*.

20. Deshpande, 'The Indian Woman – Myths, Stereotypes and the Reality'.

21. Menon, 263.

22. *Publisher's Weekly*, 31 May 1999.
23. Futehally, review of *A Matter of Time*.
24. Lakshmi Mani, review of *A Matter of Time, India Currents*, August 1999.
25. Meena Nayak, review of *A Matter of Time, World View*, 12:4, November 1999.
26. Maureen Mclane, review of *A Matter of Time, New York Times Book Review*, 8 August 1999.
27 Vrinda Nabar, 'Words ... Language ... and Truth', *Sunday Observer*, 9 April 2000.

CHAPTER 6. SMALL REMEDIES

1. Shashi Deshpande, 'No (Hu)man is an Island', *The Times of India*, 23 April 1992.
2. Ritu Menon, 'Pentimento', *The Book Review*, July 2000, 24–5.
3. Shashi Deshpande, interview with Sudipta Datta, *Express Magazine*, 5 December 1999, 4.
4. Shashi Deshpande, quoted by Vrinda Nabar, 'Words ... Language ... and Truth', *Sunday Observer*, 9 April 2000.
5. Shashi Deshpande, *Small Remedies* (New Delhi: Penguin India, 2000), 284. All quotations are from this text.
6. At a most unusual performance at the NIAS, Bangalore, on 13 January 2001 by the Little Theatre Group, Hyderabad, which gave a musical recital accompanied by readings of appropriate passages from *Small Remedies*.
7. Deshpande, quoted by Nabar, 'Words ... Language ... and Truth'.
8. Deshpande, 'The Indian Woman – Myths, Stereotypes and the Reality'.
9. C. S. Lakshmi, *The Singer and the Song: Conversations with Women Musicians* (New Delhi: Kali for Women, 2000), viii.
10. The contempt and ridicule Bai may have had to face can be surmised from many first-person narratives by women who dared to 'cross the threshold'. See for example Rushsundari Debi's attempts to learn to read and write, in Tanika Sarkar's *Words to Win: The Making of 'Amar Jiban'*.
11. Deshpande, 'The Indian Woman – Myths, Stereotypes and the Reality'.
12. Ibid.

CHAPTER 7. CONCLUSION

1. Quoted in Meenakshi Mukherjee's *The Perishable Empire: Essays in Indian Writing in English* (New Delhi: Oxford University Press, 2000), 3.
2. See Gauri Visvanathan, *Masks of Conquest: Literary Study and British Rule in India* (1989; New Delhi: Oxford University Press, 1998), 3.
3. See Visvanathan, *Masks of Conquest*, 3. All quotations are from 'Midnight's Orphans' by Sheela Reddy.
4. Shashi Deshpande, 'English, S Inter Alia', *Outlook*, 11 March 2002, 59.
5. Shashi Deshpande, 'Them and Us', in Shirley Chew and Anna Rutherford (eds.), *Unbecoming Daughters of the Empire* (Sydney: Dangaroo Press, 1993).
6. Ibid.
7. Ibid.
8. Deshpande, 'Of Concerns, Of Anxieties', 104.
9. Ibid.
10. Ibid.
11. Ibid.
12. Shashi Deshpande, 'Where Do We Belong?: Regional, National, or International' (unpublished article, August 2002).
13. In Choudhury, 'Interview with Shashi Deshpande', 17.
14. Deshpande, 'Of Concerns and Anxieties'.
15. Deshpande, 'Where Do We Belong?'.
16. Ibid.
17. Ibid.

Select Bibliography

WORKS BY SHASHI DESHPANDE

Novels

The Dark Holds No Terrors (New Delhi: Vikas Publishing House, 1980; repr. Penguin India, 1990, 1993).
Come up and be Dead (New Delhi: Vikas Publishing House, 1982); repub. Dronequill Publishers, 2003.
If I Die Today (New Delhi: Vikas Publishing House, 1982).
Roots and Shadows (New Delhi: Orient Longmans, 1983).
That Long Silence (London: Virago Press, 1988; repr. Penguin India, 1989).
The Binding Vine (London: Virago Press, 1993; repr. Penguin India, 1993).
A Matter of Time (New Delhi: Penguin India, 1996; New York: Feminist Press at the City University of New York, 1999 – includes an Afterword, 'No Longer Silent', by Ritu Menon).
Small Remedies (New Delhi: Viking by Penguin India, 2000).

Short Stories

The Legacy (Calcutta: Writers Workshop, 1978).
It was Dark (Calcutta: Writers Workshop, 1986).
It was the Nightingale (Calcutta: Writers Workshop, 1986).
The Miracle and Other Stories (Calcutta: Writers Workshop, 1986).
The Intrusion and Other Stories (New Delhi: Penguin India, 1993).
The Stone Women (Calcutta: Writers Workshop, 2000).
Collected Stories, vol. 1, Preface by the author, and Foreword by Amrita Bhalla (New Delhi: Penguin India, 2003).
Collected Stories, vol. 2 (New Delhi: Penguin India, 2004).

Children's Books

A Summer Adventure (New Delhi: India Book House, 1978).
The Hidden Treasure (New Delhi: India Book House, 1980).

The Only Witness (New Delhi: India Book House, 1980).

The Narayanpur Incident (New Delhi: India Book House, 1992; repr. Penguin India 1995).

Shashi Deshpande's works have been translated into German, Italian, Dutch, Finnish.

Essays and Articles

'The Indian Woman – Myths, Stereotypes and the Reality', private papers, 1977. An adaptation is published as the Afterword in Shashi Deshpande's *The Stone Women* (Calcutta: Writers Workshop, 2000).

'The Writing of a Novel, in *Indian Women Novelists*, ed. R. K. Dhawan (New Delhi: Prestige Books, 1991), 31–6.

'No (Hu)man is an Island', *The Times of India*, 23 April 1992.

'An Archipelago', *Indian Review of Books*, 3:1 (16 October–15 November 1993), 32–3.

'Them and Us', in Shirley Chew and Anne Rutherford (eds.), *Unbecoming Daughters of the Empire* (Sydney: Dangaroo Press, 1993).

'Language No Bar', *Sunday Times*, 23 April 1995.

'Literature Should Know No Barriers', *Telegraph*, 30 August 1995.

'Is this the Promised Land?', *Telegraph*, 24 July 1996.

'Of Concerns, Of Anxieties', Indian Literature: Women's Writing in English, *New Voices*, 175, 39:5 (September–October 1996), 103–10.

'Where Do We Belong? The "Problem" of English in India', *Kunapipi: Journal of Post-Colonial Writing*, 19:3 (1997), 65–74.

'The Dilemma of the Woman Writer', in *The Fiction of Shashi Deshpande*, ed. R. S. Pathak (New Delhi: Creative Books, 1998).

'Writing from the Margin', *The Book Review*, 22:3 (March 1998).

'Dear Reader', *Indian Review of Books*, 16 February–15 March 2000, 21–4.

'Seeking a Moral Base', *Hindu Literary Review*, 4 February 2001.

'English, S Inter Alia' *Outlook*, 11 March 2002, 59.

'Where Do We Belong: Regional, National or International', private papers (unpublished, 2002).

'The Writer as Activist', *Hindu Literary Review*, 6 July 2003.

Writing from the Margin and other essays (New Delhi: Penguin/Viking, 2003).

SELECTED INTERVIEWS WITH SHASHI DESHPANDE

Carvalho, Stanley, 'Everyone Has a Right to Choose a Language', *Sunday Observer*, February 1990.

Choudhury, Romita, 'Interview with Shashi Deshpande', *World Literature Written in English*, 34:2 (1995).

Dasgupta, Uma Mahadevan, interview with Shashi Deshpande, *Hindu Literary Review*, 4 November 2001.

Dickman, Sue, 'In Conversation: Sue Dickman with Indian Women Writers', *The Book Review*, 19:4 (April 1995), 30–35.

Gangadharan, Geetha, 'Denying the Otherness', *Indian Communicator*, 20 November 1994.

Holm, Chandra, interview with Shashi Deshpande, 30 October 1997. Website <http://www.dharwad.com/nimmaputa/shashi.html>

Holmström, Lakshmi, interview with Shashi Deshpande, *Wasafiri*, 17 (Spring 1993), 22–7.

Nair, Hema, interview with Shashi Deshpande, <Little India.com>, October 1999.

Riti, M. D., 'There's No Looking Back for Shashi Deshpande', *Eve's Weekly*, 18–24 (June 1988), 26–8.

Sudipta, Datta, interview with Shashi Deshpande, *Express Magazine*, 5 December 1999, 4.

Viswanathan, Vanmala, 'A Woman's World . . . All the Way', *Literature Alive*, 1:3 (December 1997), 8–14.

CRITICAL STUDIES

There are few critical studies on the novels of Shashi Deshpande. The following include full-length studies or articles in books and journals. Her novels and short stories have been reviewed in leading newspapers and journals.

Dhawan, R. K. (ed.), *Indian Women Novelists* (New Delhi: Prestige Books, 1991). This is a 5-volume work, with articles on Deshpande in almost every volume.

Jain, Jasbir, and Amina Amin (eds), *Margins of Erasure: Purdah in the Subcontinental Novel in English* (New Delhi: Sterling Publishers, 1995). Contains articles on Deshpande: Rani Dharkar, 'Marriage as Purdah: Fictional Rendering of a Social Reality' (pp. 49–59) and Kamini Dinesh, 'Moving Out of the Cloistered Self: Shashi Deshpande's Protagonists' (pp. 196–205).

Kirpal, Viney (ed.), *The New Indian Novel in English: A Study of the 1980's* (New Delhi: Allied, 1990). Contains Adele King's 'Shashi Deshpande: Portraits of an Indian Woman' (pp. 159–68).

Michel, Martina, Sybille Kuster, Liselotte Glage, Helga Ritter and Beatrix Thomasi, 'Indian Women between Tradition and Self-Determination: Problems in the Reception of Indo-English Short

Stories Written by Women', in *Mediating Cultures* (Essen: Blaue Eule, 1991), 1–22.

Nayak, K. Kishori, 'The Diaries of a Sane House-Wife': Shashi Deshpande's *That Long Silence*, in Indian Literature: Women's Writing in English, *New Voices*, 175, 39:5 (September–October 1996), 111–19.

Pathak, R. S. (ed.), *Recent Indian Fiction* (New Delhi: Prestige Books, 1994). Articles on Shashi Deshpande include Bijay Kumar Das, 'Shashi Deshpande's *That Long Silence* and the Question of the Reader Response' (pp. 202–9).

——(ed.), *The Fiction of Shashi Deshpande* (New Delhi: Creative Books, 1998).

Rajan, Rajeswari Sunder, 'The Feminist Plot and the Nationalist Allegory: Homa (Home) and World in Two Indian Women's Novels in English, *Modern Fiction Studies*, 39 (Spring 1993), 71–92.

Rajeshwar, M., 'The Trauma of a House-Wife: A Psychological Study of Shashi Deshpande's *That Long Silence*', *Commomnwealth Quarterly*, 17:43 (June–September 1991), 41–61.

Reimenschneider, Dieter, 'Indian Women Writing in English: The Short Story', *World Literature Written in English*, 25:2 (1985), 312–18.

Sandhu, Sarabjit, *The Image of Women in the Novels of Shashi Deshpande* (New Delhi: Prestige Books, 1991).

Singh, Sushila (ed,), *Feminism and Recent Fiction in English* (New Delhi: Prestige Books, 1991). Includes P. Ramamoorthi's ' "My Life is My Own": A Study of Shashi Deshpande's Women' (pp. 115–127), and Sarla Palkar's 'Breaking the Silence: Shashi Deshpande's *That Long Silence*' (pp. 163–9).

Suneel, Seema, *Man–Woman Relationship in Indian Fiction* (New Delhi: Prestige, 1995). See pp. 20–73 and pp. 74–122.

BACKGROUND READING

Ahmad, Aijaz, *In Theory:Classes, Nations, Literatures* (London: Verso, 1992).

Appachana, Anjana, *Listening Now*, (New York: Random House, 1998; New Delhi: IndiaInk, 1998).

Ashcroft, Bill, Gareth Griffiths and Helen Tiffin, *The Empire Writes Back: Theory and Practice in Post-Colonial Literatures* (London: Routledge, 1989).

Ashcroft, Bill, Gareth Griffiths and Helen Tiffin (eds), *The Post Colonial Studies Reader* (London: Routledge, 1995).

Baldwin, Shauna Singh, *What the Body Remembers* (New Delhi: HarperCollins, 1999).

Basu, Amrita (ed.), *The Challenge of Local Feminisms: Women's Movements in Global Perspective* (Westview Press, 1995; New Delhi: Kali for Women, 1999).

Basu, Aparna, and Bharati Ray (eds), *From Independence towards Freedom: Indian Women since 1947* (New Delhi: Oxford University Press, 1999).

Bhabha, Homi, *The Location of Culture* (London: Routledge, 1994).

Bhasin, Kamla, *Understanding Gender* (New Delhi: Kali for Women, 2000).

——*What is Patriarchy?* (New Delhi: Kali for Women, 1993).

Bhasin, Kamla, and Nighat Said Khan, *Some Questions on Feminism and its Relevance in South Asia* (New Delhi: Kali for Women, 1986).

Dhammapada, The, trans. Narada Thera (London: John Murray, 1954).

Eagleton, Mary (ed.), *Feminist Literary Theory: A Reader* (Oxford: Blackwell Publishers, 1986).

Forbes, Geraldine, *The New Cambridge History of India,* vol. 4, no. 2, *Women in Modern India* (Cambridge: Cambridge University Press, 1998).

Holmström, Lakshmi (ed.), *The Inner Courtyard: Stories by Indian Women* (London: Virago Press, 1990).

Humm, Maggie (ed.), *Feminisms: A Reader* (London: Harvester Wheatsheaf, 1992).

Jain, Jasbir, *Gendered Realities, Human Spaces: The Writings of Shashi Deshpande* (New Delhi: Rawat, 2003).

Kapur, Manju, ' "Writing", "Span" ', Special Literary Section, *Indian and American Writers*, January–February 2002.

Kumar, Radha, *The History of Doing: An Illustrated Account of Movements for Women's Rights and Feminism in India,1800–1900* (New Delhi: Kali for Women, 1993).

Lal, Malashri, *The Law of the Threshold: Women Writers in Indian English* (Shimla: Indian Institute of Advanced Study, 1995).

Lal, Malashri, Alamgir Hashmi and Victor J. Ramraj (eds), *Post-Independence Voices in South Asian Writings* (New Delhi: Doaba House, 2001).

Lakshmi, C. S., *The Singer and the Song: Conversations with Women Musicians* (New Delhi: Kali for Women, 2000).

Loomba, Ania, *Colonialism/Postcolonialism* (London and New York: Routledge, 1998).

Moers, Ellen, *Literary Women* (London: W. H. Allen, 1977).

Mohanty, Chandra Talpade, 'Feminist Encounters: Locating the Politics of Experience', in *Destabilizing Theory: Contemporary Feminist*

Debates, ed. Michele Barrett and Anne Phillips (Stanford: Stanford University Press, 1992).

Mukherjee, Meenakshi, *The Perishable Empire: Essays on Indian Writing in English* (New Delhi: Oxford University Press, 2000).

Mukherjee, Meenakshi, *The Twice Born Fiction: Themes and Techniques of the Indian Novel in English* (London: Heinemann, 1971).

——(ed.), *Early Novels in India* (New Delhi: Sahitya Akademi, 2002).

——(ed.), with Harish Trivedi), *Interrogating Postcolonialism: Theory, Text and Context* (Shimla: Indian Institute of Advanced Study, 1996).

Nabar, Vrinda, *Caste as Woman* (New Delhi: Penguin Books, 1995).

Narayan, R. K., *The Indian Epics Retold: The Ramayana, The Mahabharata, Gods, Demons and Others* (New Delhi: Penguin Books, 2000).

Principal Upanishad, The, ed. S. Radhakrishnan (London: George Allen & Unwin, 1953).

Rajan, Rajeswari Sunder, 'Writing in English in India, Again', *Hindu Literary Review*, 18 and 25 February, 2001.

Reddy, Sheela, 'Midnight's Orphans', in *Outlook*, 25 February 2002, 54–62.

Rushdie, Salman, *Imaginary Homelands: Essays and Criticism 1981–1991* (London: Granta Books, 1991).

Rushdie, Salman, and Elizabeth West (eds), *The Vintage Book of Indian Writing 1947–1997* (London: Vintage, 1997).

Said, Edward W., *Orientalism* (London: Routledge & Kegan Paul, 1978).

——*Culture and Imperialism* (New York: Vintage, 1994).

Sangari, Kumkum, and Sudesh Vaid (eds), *Recasting Women: Essays in Colonial History* (New Delhi: Kali for Women, 1989).

Sarkar, Tanika, and Urvashi Butalia (eds), *Women and the Hindu Right: A Collection of Essays* (New Delhi: Kali for Women, 1995).

Sarkar, Tanika, *Words to Win: The Making of 'Amar Jiban' – A Modern Autobiography* (New Delhi: Kali for Women, 1999).

Satthianadhan, Krupabai, *Saguna: The First Autobiographical Novel in English by an Indian Woman* (1895; New Delhi: Oxford University Press, 1998).

Sen, Amartya, 'The Indian Identity: Neither Singular nor Fragile', Dorab Tata Memorial Lecture, New Delhi, 26 February 2001; in *The Times of India*, 3 March 2001.

Singh, Namvar, 'Decolonising the Indian Mind', *Indian Literature*, 151 (September–October 1992).

Sinha, Mrinalini, *Colonial Masculinity: The 'Manly Englishman' and the 'Effeminate Bengali' in the Late Nineteenth Century* (1995; New Delhi: Kali for Women, 1997).

Showalter, Elaine, *A Literature of their Own: British Women Novelists from Brontë to Lessing* (London: Virago Press, 1982).

Sorabji, Cornelia, *India Calling: The Memories of Cornelia Sorabji, India's First Woman Barrister* (1934; New Delhi: Oxford University Press, 2001).

'Stree': A Tribute to the Indian Woman', a collectors' edition of *Outlook* (n.d.).

Spivak, Gayatri Chakravorty, 'Can the Subaltern Speak?', in C. Nelson and L. Grossberg (eds), *Marxism and the Interpretation of Culture* (Basingstoke: Macmillan Education, 1988).

——*The Post-Colonial Critic: Interviews, Strategies, Dialogues*, ed. Sarah Harasym (New York: Routledge, Chapman & Hall, 1990).

Suleri, Sara, 'Woman Skin Deep: Feminism and the Postcolonial Condition', *Critical Enquiry*, 18 (Summer 1992).

Tagore, Rabindranath, *The Home and the World*, trans. Surendranath Tagore (1st pub. in Bengali, 1916; New Delhi: Penguin, 1999).

Tharu, Susie, and K. Lalita (eds), *Women Writing in India: 600 B.C. to the Present*, vol. 2, *The Twentieth Century* (New Delhi: Oxford University Press, 1993).

Viswanathan, Gauri, *Masks of Conquest: Literary Study and British Rule in India* (1989; New Delhi: Oxford University Press, 1998).

Wasi, Jehanara (ed), *A Storehouse of Tales: Contemporary Indian Women Writers* (New Delhi: Srishti, 2001).

Zide, Arlene (ed.), *In Their Own Voice: The Penguin Anthology of Contemporary Indian Women Poets* (New Delhi: Penguin, 1993).

Index

*Recent and
Forthcoming Titles
in the
New Series of*

WRITERS AND
THEIR WORK

WRITERS AND THEIR WORK

RECENT & FORTHCOMING TITLES

Title	Author
Chinua Achebe	*Nahem Yousaf*
Peter Ackroyd	*Susana Onega*
Kingsley Amis	*Richard Bradford*
Anglo-Saxon Verse	*Graham Holderness*
Antony and Cleopatra 2/e	*Ken Parker*
As You Like It	*Penny Gay*
W. H. Auden	*Stan Smith*
Jane Austen	*Robert Miles*
Alan Ayckbourn	*Michael Holt*
J. G. Ballard	*Michel Delville*
Pat Barker	*Sharon Monteith*
Djuna Barnes	*Deborah Parsons*
Julian Barnes	*Matthew Pateman*
Samuel Beckett	*Sinead Mooney*
Aphra Behn 2/e	*S. J. Wiseman*
John Betjeman	*Dennis Brown*
William Blake	*Steven Vine*
Edward Bond	*Michael Mangan*
Anne Brontë	*Betty Jay*
Emily Brontë	*Stevie Davies*
A. S. Byatt	*Richard Todd*
Byron	*Drummond Bone*
Caroline Drama	*Julie Sanders*
Angela Carter 2/e	*Lorna Sage*
Bruce Chatwin	*Kerry Featherstone*
Geoffrey Chaucer	*Steve Ellis*
Children's Literature	*Kimberley Reynolds*
Caryl Churchill 2/e	*Elaine Aston*
John Clare	*John Lucas*
S. T. Coleridge	*Stephen Bygrave*
Joseph Conrad	*Cedric Watts*
Coriolanus	*Anita Pacheco*
Stephen Crane	*Kevin Hayes*
Crime Fiction	*Martin Priestman*
Anita Desai	*Elaine Ho*
Shashi Deshpande	*Armrita Bhalla*
Charles Dickens	*Rod Mengham*
John Donne	*Stevie Davies*
Margaret Drabble	*Glenda Leeming*
John Dryden	*David Hopkins*
Carol Ann Duffy 2/e	*Deryn Rees Jones*
Douglas Dunn	*David Kennedy*
Early Modern Sonneteers	*Michael Spiller*
George Eliot	*Josephine McDonagh*
T. S. Eliot	*Colin MacCabe*
English Translators of Homer	*Simeon Underwood*
J. G. Farrell	*John McLeod*
Henry Fielding	*Jenny Uglow*
Veronica Forrest-Thomson – Language Poetry	*Alison Mark*
E. M. Forster	*Nicholas Royle*
John Fowles	*William Stephenson*
Brian Friel	*Geraldine Higgins*
Athol Fugard	*Dennis Walder*
Elizabeth Gaskell	*Kate Flint*

RECENT & FORTHCOMING TITLES

Title	Author
The *Gawain*-Poet	*John Burrow*
The Georgian Poets	*Rennie Parker*
William Golding 2/e	*Kevin McCarron*
Graham Greene	*Peter Mudford*
Neil M. Gunn	*J. B. Pick*
Ivor Gurney	*John Lucas*
Hamlet 2/e	*Ann Thompson & Neil Taylor*
Thomas Hardy 2/e	*Peter Widdowson*
Tony Harrison	*Joe Kelleher*
William Hazlitt	*J. B. Priestley; R. L. Brett (intro. by Michael Foot)*
Seamus Heaney 2/e	*Andrew Murphy*
George Herbert	*T.S. Eliot (intro. by Peter Porter)*
Geoffrey Hill	*Andrew Roberts*
Gerard Manley Hopkins	*Daniel Brown*
Henrik Ibsen 2/e	*Sally Ledger*
Kazuo Ishiguro 2/e	*Cynthia Wong*
Henry James – The Later Writing	*Barbara Hardy*
James Joyce 2/e	*Steven Connor*
Julius Caesar	*Mary Hamer*
Franz Kafka	*Michael Wood*
John Keats	*Kelvin Everest*
James Kelman	*Gustav Klaus*
Rudyard Kipling	*Jan Montefiore*
Hanif Kureishi	*Ruvani Ranasinha*
Samuel Johnson	*Liz Bellamy*
William Langland: *Piers Plowman*	*Claire Marshall*
King Lear	*Terence Hawkes*
Philip Larkin 2/e	*Laurence Lerner*
D. H. Lawrence	*Linda Ruth Williams*
Doris Lessing	*Elizabeth Maslen*
C. S. Lewis	*William Gray*
Wyndham Lewis and Modernism	*Andrzej Gasiorak*
David Lodge	*Bernard Bergonzi*
Katherine Mansfield	*Andrew Bennett*
Christopher Marlowe	*Thomas Healy*
Andrew Marvell	*Annabel Patterson*
Ian McEwan 2/e	*Kiernan Ryan*
Measure for Measure	*Kate Chedgzoy*
The Merchant of Venice	*Warren Chernaik*
Middleton and his Collaborators	*Hutchings & Bromham*
A Midsummer Night's Dream	*Helen Hacket*
John Milton	*Nigel Smith*
Alice Munro	*Ailsa Cox*
Vladimir Nabokov	*Neil Cornwell*
V. S. Naipaul	*Suman Gupta*
New Woman Writers	*Marion Shaw/Lyssa Randolph*
Grace Nichols	*Sarah Lawson-Welsh*
Edna O'Brien	*Amanda Greenwood*
Flann O'Brien	*Joe Brooker*
Ben Okri	*Robert Fraser*
George Orwell	*Douglas Kerr*
Othello	*Emma Smith*
Walter Pater	*Laurel Brake*
Brian Patten	*Linda Cookson*
Caryl Phillips	*Helen Thomas*

RECENT & FORTHCOMING TITLES

Title	Author
Harold Pinter	*Mark Batty*
Sylvia Plath 2/e	*Elisabeth Bronfen*
Pope Amongst the Satirists	*Brean Hammond*
Revenge Tragedies of the Renaissance	*Janet Clare*
Jean Rhys 2/e	*Helen Carr*
Richard II	*Margaret Healy*
Richard III	*Edward Burns*
Dorothy Richardson	*Carol Watts*
John Wilmot, Earl of Rochester	*Germaine Greer*
Romeo and Juliet	*Sasha Roberts*
Christina Rossetti	*Kathryn Burlinson*
Salman Rushdie 2/e	*Damian Grant*
Paul Scott	*Jacqueline Banerjee*
The Sensation Novel	*Lyn Pykett*
P. B. Shelley	*Paul Hamilton*
Sir Walter Scott	*Harriet Harvey Wood*
Iain Sinclair	*Robert Sheppard*
Christopher Smart	*Neil Curry*
Wole Soyinka	*Mpalive Msiska*
Muriel Spark	*Brian Cheyette*
Edmund Spenser	*Colin Burrow*
Gertrude Stein	*Nicola Shaughnessy*
Laurence Sterne	*Manfred Pfister*
Bram Stoker	*Andrew Maunder*
Graham Swift	*Peter Widdowson*
Jonathan Swift	*Ian Higgins*
Swinburne	*Catherine Maxwell*
Elizabeth Taylor	*N. R. Reeve*
Alfred Tennyson	*Seamus Perry*
W. M. Thackeray	*Richard Salmon*
D. M. Thomas	*Bran Nicol*
Three Lyric Poets	*William Rowe*
J. R. R. Tolkien	*Charles Moseley*
Leo Tolstoy	*John Bayley*
Charles Tomlinson	*Tim Clark*
Anthony Trollope	*Andrew Sanders*
Victorian Quest Romance	*Robert Fraser*
Marina Warner	*Laurence Coupe*
Irvine Welsh	*Berthold Schoene*
Edith Wharton	*Janet Beer*
Oscar Wilde	*Alexandra Warrick*
Angus Wilson	*Peter Conradi*
Mary Wollstonecraft	*Jane Moore*
Women's Gothic 2/e	*E. J. Clery*
Women Poets of the 19th Century	*Emma Mason*
Women Romantic Poets	*Anne Janowitz*
Women Writers of Children's Classics	*Mary Sebag-Montefiore*
Women Writers of the 17th Century	*Ramona Wray*
Virginia Woolf 2/e	*Laura Marcus*
Working Class Fiction	*Ian Haywood*
W. B. Yeats	*Edward Larrissy*
Charlotte Yonge	*Alethea Hayter*

TITLES IN PREPARATION

Title	Author
Fleur Adcock	*Janet Wilson*
Ama Ata Aidoo	*Nana Wilson-Tagoe*
Matthew Arnold	*Kate Campbell*
Margaret Atwood	*Marion Wynne-Davies*
John Banville	*Peter Dempsey*
William Barnes	*Christopher Ricks*
Black British Writers	*Deidre Osborne*
Charlotte Brontë	*Stevie Davies*
Robert Browning	*John Woodford*
Basil Bunting	*Martin Stannard*
John Bunyan	*Tamsin Spargoe*
Cymbeline	*Peter Swaab*
David Edgar	*Peter Boxall*
Nadine Gordimer	*Lewis Nkosi*
Geoffrey Grigson	*R. M. Healey*
David Hare	*Jeremy Ridgman*
Ted Hughes	*Susan Bassnett*
The Imagist Poets	*Andrew Thacker*
Ben Jonson	*Anthony Johnson*
A. L. Kennedy	*Dorothy McMillan*
Jack Kerouac	*Michael Hrebebiak*
Jamaica Kincaid	*Susheila Nasta*
Rosamond Lehmann	*Judy Simon*
Una Marson & Louise Bennett	*Alison Donnell*
Norman MacCaig	*Alasdair Macrae*
Much Ado About Nothing	*John Wilders*
R. K. Narayan	*Shirley Chew*
Ngugi wa Thiong'o	*Brendon Nicholls*
Religious Poets of the 17th Century	*Helen Wilcox*
Samuel Richardson	*David Deeming*
Olive Schreiner	*Carolyn Burdett*
Sam Selvon	*Ramchand & Salick*
Olive Senior	*Denise de Canes Narain*
Mary Shelley	*Catherine Sharrock*
Charlotte Smith & Helen Williams	*Angela Keane*
R. L. Stevenson	*David Robb*
Tom Stoppard	*Nicholas Cadden*
Dylan Thomas	*Chris Wiggington*
Three Avant-Garde Poets	*Peter Middleton*
Derek Walcott	*Stephen Regan*